MW00745348

Bryan Fiese's

NO TEACHER LEFT BEHIND

Keeping Up with and Captivating "Generation Next" in the Classroom

2nd Edition

By: Bryan Fiese

Published By:

Printed in the United States of America by
Motivated Proformance, Inc.

Cover Design:
Motivated Proformance, Inc.

Edited:
Greg Levin
Nancy French
David Fried

Library of Congress Number:

ISBN # 978-0-9818525-3-9

Table of Contents

SECTION I
GENERATION NEXT & ALL THE REST

YOU CAN'T TEACH A NEW STUDENT OLD TRICKS. OR AT LEAST YOU SHOULDN'T IF YOU EXPECT TO CONNECT WITH, ENGAGE AND TRULY INSPIRE HIM.

Chapter 1
How Things
Have Changed

Understanding the Generations

You can't teach a new student old tricks. Or at least you shouldn't if you expect to connect with, engage and truly inspire him.

Today's teens and pre-teens – members of what's been called "Generation Next" (a.k.a., "Generation Y" or the "Millenials") – have grown up in a very different world than the vast majority of educators in today's elementary schools, high schools, colleges and universities. Members of Generation Next – born in the mid-1980s and 1990s – have postmodern sensibilities, lightning quick minds and short attention spans. They covet technology, using it extensively not only to learn about the world and to entertain themselves, but to communicate with one another. This is a unique and advanced crew – one that is not likely to be moved or motivated by the educational methods of yesterday.

The title of this book says it all: "No Teacher Left Behind." The script has flipped. With such highly active, independent, impatient, creative, intelligent and demanding minds filling today's classrooms, it is now the teachers who are, in a sense, at risk of being left in the academic dust. Gone are the days when teachers could educate and command respect by ruling with an iron fist. "Motivation via intimidation" no longer works. With Generation Next, we have reached the Age of Empowerment. These individuals seek coaches and mentors, not autocrats. Thus, educators who continue to cling tightly to traditional teaching tactics, theories and philosophies will fail.

This is not to say that today's teachers must bend over backwards and do whatever their students demand; no, the teacher must still steer the ship. However, the successful educator will take the time to fully understand the complexities and collective consciousness of this remarkable and confounding generation, then strategically adapt their teaching approach to create a powerful learning environment.

William Strauss and Neil Howe, noted experts on generational studies, have dubbed Generation Next "the next great generation" – not just based on the sheer size of this group, but based on the pragmatic and proactive mindset that, in general, defines these individuals. However, true greatness cannot be achieved without great educators – confident leaders and mentors who can fully tap and help direct the promising potential of today's youth.

And that's where you come in.

THE GENERATIONS

We have evolved with each passing generation, and for the first time in American history, we have four clearly distinct generations working side-by-side in our schools. Each generation brings their own beliefs, ideas, emotions and commotion. To help better understand Generation Next, it is important to compare and contrast it with the other generations with which Next coexists.

5

Veteran Generation – 1922-1946

This generation – approximately 44 million strong – has also been referred to as the "Greatest Generation," as its members collectively anchored a lot of the values that are woven into American society. Most "veterans" subscribe to a "scarcity mentality," with the dark and dank Great Depression days still caged in their subconscious minds.

This is a very dedicated and loyal generation, where most people are/were grateful just to have a job. They entered into a new position with the idea they would stick with that company until retirement. They grew up with a clear chain of command: You were either the boss or did what the boss said – no questions. It was a period where, unlike today, managers were always older than those whom they managed. Business deals were made on a handshake, and your word meant more than anything.

With regard to the education of the Veteran Generation, the teacher was dictator. Corporal punishment was in full force, and students knew to sit up straight, pay attention and not talk out of turn.

One of the negatives with regard to this generation is that their parents, generally speaking, did not openly show emotion to or elicit emotion from the children. For the most part, the child was there to serve the parents and didn't have a voice – the classic "be seen and not heard" scenario. Children knew they were doing alright if they didn't get backhanded.

One of the greatest attributes of members of the Veteran Generation is their interpersonal communication

Disclaimer: Generalizations about Generations

Making generalizations about an entire generation is a risky endeavor. No group of people can be perfectly pigeon-holed, neatly summed up by a set of sweeping statements and descriptions. Naturally, within each generation, there is a vast amount of diversity.

That being said, rigorous research over decades has helped to uncover certain core tendencies and characteristics that predominate in a given generational group, and has helped us to understand why people within a given group tend to think and behave as they do. This book does not aim to create or promote rigid stereotypes, or to oversimplify complex social issues; rather, it aims to assist ambitious, dedicated educators in their effort to better understand, inspire and learn from the generation that sits before them in the classroom or lecture hall, each day eager to find their place in, and ideally change, the world.

skills. They value and enjoy conversation and organic dialogue – one-on-one with individuals. They are baffled by today's obsession with email, chat, cell phones and video games. And while they may toy around a bit with such technologies, they feel sorry for those who, in their eyes, have become slaves to such communication tools.

BABY BOOMERS – 1946-1964

"Baby Boomers" refers to the 76 million people who quickly began to populate the planet in the years immediately following World War II. It was the first generation to be raised on television and was largely impacted by the Vietnam War. It was also the first generation to seek a higher consciousness and self-actualization. Boomers broke the family tradition by challenging their very existence. They coveted education and were free spirits who viewed free love, sex, drugs and rock-n-roll as a celebration of their freedom and growth.

As parents, most Boomers simmered down and created a highly nurturing environment for their children, enjoyed planning family outings and activities and strongly encouraged personal expression. With their "Baby on Board" signs fixed to their cars and their disposable income, Boomers were labeled the "yuppie" generation.

Even though boomers took a different path than their parents had, they still maintained the same traditional values and beliefs concerning friends, work and education.

Boomers are independent thinkers who take a tremendous amount of responsibility for their own success. Their independence and self-reliance can be largely attributed to the fact that they have watched their job loyalty get rewarded with layoffs from increasingly faceless organizations.

While they hold face-to-face communication in high regard (and often use body language when communicating), Boomers are not averse to technology. Most have adapted well to using the technology that drives modern communication.

With people living so much longer today, many Boomers find themselves in the interesting and challenging position of caring for their elderly parents as well as their own children.

GENERATION X – 1965-1981

"Generation X" is generally known for its lack of optimism for the future, nihilism, cynicism, skepticism, alienation and mistrust of traditional values. During the early 1990s, the media portrayed Generation X as a group of flannel-wearing, McJob-working, alienated, overeducated, under-achieving slackers more concerned about body piercings than building a resume. While there was some truth in this portrayal, the Xer image was based largely on rigid stereotypes. Helping to fuel such stereotypes was a book called *Generation X: Tales for an Accelerated Culture*, written by Douglas Coupland in 1991. You couldn't pick up a magazine or turn to a newscast without reading about or witnessing the media slamming Generation X and their less than stellar work ethic. Reactionary statements like, "Imagine a world of Slackers running this country" became commonplace. Xers grew up watching MTV, playing video games and coming home to an empty house after school ("latchkey kids") – with both parents (or their single parent) working. Consequently, they became very independent at an early age.

Much like their parents had in the 1970s, Xers sought out change. They watched their Baby Boomer moms and dads dedicate their lives to work and the corporation only to get laid off in the latter years of their career due to downsizing and restructuring. Naturally, such callous and cold treatment of their parents engendered in Xers a mistrust of corporate America and traditional views of work. Their "live first and work second" mantra had a profound impact on big business, forcing corporations to revisit and revamp their recruiting, hiring and staffing strategies. In order to attract and engage Xers, companies began offering more flex time, co-op teaching and telecommuting, as well as daycare facilities on site.

Bill Clinton put it best when he said, this is "not a generation of slackers but a generation of seekers." Xers have contributed more to our society than any other generation to date. By challenging the status quo, embracing technology and asserting their fierce independence, they helped to transform the way we teach, work and live.

GENERATION NEXT – 1982-2000

Generation Next (a.k.a., "Millennials") is a fast and fearless generation that has grown up with technology their entire lives. Remember the "No Fear" bumper stickers that were plastered on every teenager's car? Gen-Nexters are a by-product of their Gen-X parents and live for the now.

This is a huge generation that will supplant the Baby Boomers in terms of size. It is also one of the most heavily marketed-to generations, with companies battling to capture its tremendous collective buying power. Once more commonly referred to as "Generation Y", these individuals will leave you wondering *why* they do what they do. Fully empowered, they believe they can accomplish anything. The older members of Generation Next show up to a job interview and when asked by the interviewer what position they are applying for, they'll look him or her in the eye and say, "Yours." No experience, no problem.

In his book, *Growing Up Digital*, business strategist and psychologist Don Tapscott coined the term "Net Generation" as an alternative moniker for Generation Next, highlighting the significance of being the first generation to grow up completely immersed in a digital and Internet-driven world.

Backing up Tapscott is recent research conducted by Reynol Junco and Jeanna Mastrodicasa, academic leadership experts and coauthors of the book, *Connecting to the Net.Generation: What Higher Education Professionals Need to Know About Today's Students*. This tandem surveyed nearly 8,000 U.S. college students to help uncover how members of Generation Next use technology to build social networks and communicate. Here are some key findings from the study:

- ▶ *97% own a computer.*
- ▶ *94% own a cell phone.*
- ▶ *76% use instant messaging, with IM users chatting an average of 80 minutes per day.*
- ▶ *15% of IM users are logged on 24 hours a day, 7 days a week.*
- ▶ *34% use websites as their primary source of news.*
- ▶ *28% own a blog and 44% read blogs.*
- ▶ *49% download music using peer-to-peer file sharing.*
- ▶ *75% of college students have a Facebook account.*
- ▶ *60% own some type of portable music and/or video device such as an iPod.*

Gen-Nexters are the true multi-taskers of the world: They can talk on their cell phone, listen to their iPod, check email, send a text message, drive the car and put on makeup all at the same time.

This generation has completely redefined what "casual day" at work or school means, with the typical Gen-Nexter sporting low-riding, ripped $150 designer jeans, a $45 faded and torn, but new, vintage t-shirt, flip flops, shaggy hair and one or more tattoos.

Not only have members of Generation Next entered into the school system knowing more about computers

and technology than many of their teachers, this is a "Ritalin Generation" with their minds going a hundred miles an hour. Needless to say, it's no simple task for educators to capture and maintain the attention and interest of their students for any length of time. Teaching *any* group of students is hard; the hurdles have been heightened for teachers of Generation Next, with having to contend with students who very well may have been up all night interacting on MySpace or Facebook and are kept awake in class only by the potent, caffeine- and taurine-packed energy drink they slugged down just before showing up.

Adding to the challenge is the fact that this generation is, generally speaking, short on a crucial skill:

the ability to communicate effectively one-on-one with others. Their over-reliance on cell phones, IM, e-mail and blogging has left a void in their lives, unbeknownst to them. Their senses have been deadened by the lack of interpersonal communication with others.

That's not to say that teaching Generation Next comes with no rewards. Quite the contrary; this is an exceptionally intelligent and enthusiastic group of individuals. If provided with the right tools and tactics, if approached and coached in the right way, Gen-Nexters will be able to accomplish remarkable things. This should be quite an exciting time for today's teachers, as they have the opportunity to help shape the eager minds that have the potential to vastly change the shape of the future – for the better.

Of course, to do so, teachers need to do more than merely read the above description of the general tendencies of Generation Next; the successful educator today needs to know exactly how to communicate with, captivate, challenge, motivate and learn from these exceptional individuals.

RESOLVE TO BE A MASTER OF CHANGE RATHER
THAN A VICTIM OF CHANGE.
- BRIAN TRACY

WHAT TO EXPECT FROM GEN-NEXTERS IN THE CLASSROOM

So what is the profile of the proto-typical Generation Next student? What should a teacher expect to see and hear from the "tweens" and teens they are tasked with educating each day? As products of our consumer-driven postmodern society, Gen-Nexters are likely to exhibit the following key characteristics in the classroom:

15

Impatience with Techno-illiteracy

As has already been highlighted, we are dealing with individuals for whom cell phones and laptops serve as an extension of their bodies – technology is a part of who they are. As such, students have little patience for teachers who seem to be "techno-illiterate" or who lack sophistication with regard to things wireless and Web-based.

That being said, it isn't technology per se that makes this generation sit up and pay attention in the classroom. While they will certainly appreciate their teacher having techno-savvy, what will truly engage today's students is interactive, experiential learning. Successful educators keep up with the latest computer trends and digital devices, and use them to supplement – but not replace – more holistic teaching approaches that incorporate tactical learning.

An Expectation of Amusement

Welcome to the *Sesame Street* and *Barney* Generation. The chorus, "Here we are now, entertain us," from Kurt Cobain's hit song could very well serve as the mantra for Nexters. This generation has been led to believe that education is supposed to be entertaining, easy and fun, according to Mark Taylor, Director of Guidance Services at Arkansas State University-Beebe. "This does not mesh well with the studious behaviors and protracted effort required to achieve a meaningful education," says Taylor, "or the lecture-based instructional methods of many instructors. Many, if not most, educators grounded in the scientific method of the modern era are increasingly at a loss to engage postmodern students effectively."

A NEED FOR INSTANT GRATIFICATION

"Give me what I want, when I want it – and I want it now" pretty much encapsulates the Generation Nexter's postmodern mentality. They have grown up in a very customer-centric, consumerist society, where options are infinite and personal needs are catered to quickly.

Unless fully engaged in school, many members of this generation will not feel compelled to spend the time and do the work necessary to earn a post-secondary degree. They need immediate rewards and recognition throughout their educational journey; otherwise, they may succumb to their impatience and entrepreneurial spirit and seek success without the benefit of a formal education. While some may succeed in such non-academic endeavors, it is certainly in the best interest of the student to receive a meaningful and inspiring education. Thus, it is in the best interest of the educator to find ways to help students meet their needs and achieve short-term goals without spoiling the student or dumbing down the curriculum.

17

APPRECIATION OF – NOT JUST TOLERANCE FOR – DIVERSITY

Because Nexters have grown up in a digital, connected world, they have been exposed to a wide array of cultures, ethnicities, races, religions and lifestyles, and as such, they tend to be very open-minded to different types of people and different ideas and beliefs. Further enhancing their acceptance and appreciation of diversity is the fact that they have grown up in an increasingly diverse America; most Nexters have had ample face-to-face contact with people of all origins and creeds.

A recent study of Generation Next by The Pew Research Center found that about half of Nexters feel that the growing number of immigrants to the U.S. strengthens the country – more than any generation. Nexters also lead the way in their support for gay marriage and acceptance of interracial dating.

Such progressiveness should inspire any educator; students today are eager to explore new ideas, to learn about different cultures and to come up with better ways to do things. Just think about the tremendously positive impact they can have on the world.

CYNICISM

While Nexters may be open-minded when it comes to different types of people and ideas, most maintain a healthy dose of cynicism regarding the world around them. This should come as no surprise, what with Nexters growing up in the wake of 9/11 and constantly being exposed to coverage of violent crime, corrupt businesses and institutions, dishonest and small-minded politicians, self-obsessed athletes and celebrities, as well as an ailing economy.

Forward-thinking educators respect the intelligence of their students enough to acknowledge and discuss such issues in class, rather than try to paint a false image of society and politics to try to protect students from harsh realities. These discussions not only help students to better understand the world around them and to express their fears and frustrations in a positive way, these discussions also go a long way toward melting away some of the aforementioned cynicism and fostering trust in the educational system and its overall value.

A FOCUS ON EFFORT OVER EXCELLENCE

As intelligent and as rigged for success as many Nexters are, teachers will still need to do a bit of hand-holding to fully engage and drive their students. Most Nexters have grown up in a highly protective, nurturing environment in which their parents and other adult mentors have treated them like perennial winners in an effort to engrain in them a high level of self-esteem. As Arkansas State's Taylor explains, "Many, if not most, may see themselves as special stars. They have played on teams and in leagues where everyone gets a trophy, even the same size trophy."

While coddling students isn't the answer, teachers need to avoid creating an environment that is overly competitive or that considers grades the only measure of achievement and success. "Adults referencing one child as being 'better' or more talented than another at anything, or making any value-based differentiation, might be frowned upon as being judgmental and not recognizing each child's unique gifts," says Taylor.

19

However, Taylor warns against inflating grades or providing undeserving praise in the face of low academic achievement, as such practices result in students entering college expecting success with little effort.

Key Points to Remember

• *The vast changes in the world from one generation to the next means that each generation tends toward certain characteristics that distinguish them from the generations that preceded them.*

• *Gen-Nexters grew up in a digital world, one that is fast-paced and changing constantly, and one in which they, themselves, have far more control over their environment than their parents did at their age.*

• *As well as being highly techno-literate, Gen-Nexters expect learning to be fun and entertaining, expect instant gratification, appreciate diversity, are somewhat cynical and are averse to highly structured, overly competitive environments.*

	Veterans	Baby Boomers	Gen-X	Gen-Nexter's
Core Values	Respect for authority	Optimism; Involve-ment	Skepticism; Fun-Informal	Extreme Fun; NO FEAR; Confidence
Education	A dream	A birthright	A way to get ahead	An incredible expense
Communication	Rotary phone; One-on-one; Write a letter	Touch-tone phone; Call me anytime	Cell phone; Call me during the day	Internet; Instant messaging; Email
Work Ethic	Hard work; Dedicated; Respect authority; Willing to sacrifice	Workaholics; Personal fulfillment	Self-Reliance; Skeptical	Multi-tasking; Entrepre-neurial; Goal-oriented
Leadership	Directive; Control	Consensual; Directive	Ask why; Skeptical	TBD
Motivation	Your experience is respected	You are valued and needed	Instant gratifica-tion; Create own rules	Working with brilliant, creative people
Feedback	No news is good news	Money; Title; Recognition	Freedom is the best reward	Meaningful work

Chapter 2
Teaching in the New Era

TEACHING THEORIES

Two popular theories of business management and motivation – called Theory X and Theory Y – are often applied to classroom management and motivation. These theories were developed by Douglas MacGregor in his 1960 book, *The Human Side of Enterprise*, and despite the years that have passed, many of the ideas and beliefs from each theory are still present in today's businesses and classrooms – unfortunately so, in some cases.

A closer look at each theory will help to reveal how educational leadership has evolved and is still evolving, and will pave the way for the introduction of a new theory – a way to approach learning and student motivation of Gen-Nexters in the Age of Empowerment.

Theory X

Theory X embodies the old school approach to education – literally. Theory X teachers assume that the typical student is unmotivated and lacks commitment. These teachers adhere to the belief that students are not dedicated to learning, want no responsibility and would rather follow than lead. Students, in these teachers' eyes, are in school solely because they have to be; not because they are engaged or interested in their education.

To overcome such an alleged lack of ambition and dedication, Theory X teachers feel they need to be tough – to whip students into shape. They implement strict rules and employ intimidation tactics to show students that "it's my way or the highway," attempting to drive desired behaviors based on the threat of punishment.

This approach to educational leadership, developed during the emergence of the industrial age in the 1930s, couldn't be more inappropriate for educating Generation Nexters, who are hard-working, highly averse to rigidity and autocratic behavior, will not show respect until respect is given to them first and who expect education to be fun and entertaining.

Theory Y

In the 1960s and 70s, as the Baby Boomers were turning into hippies and Gen-Xers were moving into the classroom, teachers slowly began to realize that kids were rebelling against authority, and more importantly, that Theory X was no longer an effective approach to learning. Over time, Theory X gave way to Theory Y, a much more organic, student-centric approach to education. This "new-school" approach has continued to evolve as we have surged deeper and deeper into the information age. Students are viewed as assets that need to be lubricated and well-maintained to ensure optimal performance, and teachers try to remove the barriers that slow or prevent students from becoming not only a solid student but a self-actualized one.

Theory Y assumes that students are ambitious, self-motivated and eager to take on responsibility. Teachers trust students to exercise self-control and to embrace autonomy and empowerment and believe that

most want to be creative and forward-thinking in the classroom – after all, the Gen-Xers who were targeted by this approach were independent latchkey kids seeking to change the world. Thus, Theory Y teachers focused less on rigid guidelines and more on freedom in learning. The leash had been loosened.

Educators who adhere to Theory Y believe it is their job not to rule with a firm hand, but to counsel, coach and mentor students to help them achieve their full potential. Individuality is explored, and valued and used to enhance the entire learning process.

Theory Y is still a very common approach to teaching, and those who use it are much more on the mark than Theory-Xers. But with Generation Next in the classroom, it's time for a new approach that satisfies all the differences in learning between this generation and the one before it.

And that brings us to…

THEORY C

Theory C is a natural outgrowth of Theory Y, but it is tailored even more to the unique characteristics of Generation Next.

Your job as a teacher today is to customize learning to each individual student.

This is a key distinction and can be a radical notion for teachers today. Whereas many of the tools from Theory Y can be applied to today's classroom, Theory Y placed little emphasis on addressing the individual needs of each student and tailoring the classroom so that they *want* to learn more.

But your job as a teacher to Generation Next is no longer to present information and pound it into kids' heads, whether they want to learn it or not. Your job is to address their "What's in it for me?" mentality in a way that expands their minds beyond the techno-saturation of their day-to-day lives.

The "C" in Theory C stands for *Coach*, and the rest of this book approaches learning from this perspective. What Gen-Nexters need more than anything else is a coach: someone to guide them, to mentor them and to motivate them to *want* to do the work.

WHAT IS A COACH?

Think of a football coach. Not the movie stereotype of the guy screaming at a bunch of high schoolers, but one you know – either in person or on TV – perhaps from your favorite football team.

What is his job description?

▶   *Recruit the best players*
▶   *Train them to improve their skill & conditioning*
▶   *Develop a game plan for each game*
▶   *Motivate the team to work harder*
▶   *Manage the assistant coaches, such that they are doing all of the above*
▶   *Always look for how to improve*
▶   *Make important game-time decisions, including who starts and what plays to run*
▶   *Act as the chief communicator on behalf of the team*

Of course, not all of these elements apply to education

– teachers don't have the luxury of recruiting their students, and most don't have assistants – but most of these elements do apply. So, let's go further into what it means to be an educational coach.

Motivating the Team

There's a funny truth about athletes: they don't have to be there. The high school athlete doesn't have to participate in that particular extra-curricular activity, the college athlete doesn't have to wake up for practice at 5 a.m. when all his classmates are waking up at Noon, and the professional athlete doesn't have to work in that particular job.

It takes an incredible amount of dedication to be a successful athlete, and the same is true of being a student. The difference is that athletes know they have a choice, and are motivated – by popularity, money, health or any other reason – to put in that dedication, whereas students often feel they don't. And when they forget why they're doing this, it is the job of the coach to remind them of the riches that await them by putting in the effort.

Training to Improve Skill & Conditioning

Athletes run through tires. They complete obstacle courses. They lift weights and run laps. Why? It's not because there are tires on the field during a football game; it's because these exercises develop the athletes in particular ways – balance, speed, strength or aerobic capacity – which then translate to game-time success.

Similarly, most people in their day-to-day lives will never need to know how to solve a quadratic equation, or in what year the Battle of Hastings took place. An effective educator today recognizes that he is simply training students in skills – like logic, or how to learn from your mistakes – that they *will* need in their day-to-day lives moving forward.

Developing a Game Plan

A coach's job is to figure out how to win each game; but more than that, his job is to create goals and measures for the entire season. Similarly, as a teacher, you are not only creating lesson plans on a day-to-day basis, but creating at the beginning of the year – and then constantly reassessing throughout the year – goals and measures for your students, your class and you as an educator.

Of course, you may not win the Super Bowl every year – no one does – but you can develop an attitude and a plan that increases your odds of success.

Communicating for the Team

Before, during and after every game, the coach is on the sidelines, in the press room or at the radio station fielding questions on behalf of the team. Sometimes, on the practice field, it is necessary to break up or mediate altercations between athletes.

As an educator, you may spend more time breaking up fights than talking to people about how amazing your class is – but there's no reason for that to be the case. Certainly, talking to the media after a win is one of the most fun parts of a coach's job, and it may be worthwhile for you to come up with creative ways to do the same.

31

The Push-Pull Approach

You can hopefully see from the above examples, how taking the approach to coach students, rather than control them, can be much more effective given the attitudes of Gen-Next students. There's one more key distinction of being a coach, which is tied closely to the motivation factor, and that's the *Push-Pull* approach.

Picture someone halfway up a climbing wall. There's a spotter – or coach – at the bottom, who's tied to the climber. Over the past several months, the coach has been training this student, who is now set to practice a frightening new move – *jumping* to the next hold.

In training the climber up until this point, the coach has been *pushing* his student – encouraging him when he needs encouragement, helping to get his adrenalin running ("One more rep! One more climb!"), and so on.

Now, as the student jumps from one hold to the next, he's got another very important job: hold on to his student so that he doesn't fall. Maybe even give a little tug on the rope to help him reach the hold for the first time.

An effective coach doesn't just *push* his students to work harder, he *pulls* them up to the next level. He takes a hands-on approach, so that the student knows he can count on his coach to be there and to be a full partner in their shared success.

This is the push-pull approach. Push your students to work hard, but make sure you're working right there beside them every step of the way.

How to Be a Theory C Teacher

Now that we've reviewed the distinctions of being a coach, let's look specifically at what it takes to be a Theory C teacher.

Theory C involves a simple yet powerful five-step process:

1) *Assess* current performance.
2) *Counsel* students who exhibit *below average* performance.
3) *Mentor* the students who exhibit *average* performance.
4) *Coach* the students who exhibit *above average* performance.
5) *Re-evaluate.*

Assess Current Performance.

The teacher carefully evaluates and assesses each student's present performance, compares it to that of the group and assigns one of the following ratings: below average, average or above average.

Counsel Students Who Exhibit *Below Average Performance.*

Counseling means that the teacher spends time working closely with students and determining if their low performance is due to a "can't do" or a "won't do" problem. The former refers to when the students doesn't know what to do and/or how to do it; the latter ("won't do") refers to when the student understands what to do and how to do it, but simply doesn't have the desire or

33

motivation to do the task(s) at hand – as is often the case with gifted students who may be bored with curricula that are too easy for them, or with students who have strong interests in particular areas, but who are disinterested in others (e.g., the math whiz who could care less about social studies; or the art student who could care less about everything else).

Once the nature of the student's poor performance is determined, the Theory C teacher devises a developmental plan to provide focused instruction and clear examples to "can't-do" students and more engaging and interesting instruction to "won't do" students.

Teachers should spend the majority of their time working with these students. While, as we'll see in a moment, it's important not to neglect the average or above average performers, those students by and large don't need or want as much one-on-one attention as the students who are struggling, so this is where you should focus most of your efforts.

It's critical to realize that all students want to succeed – even the ones who

---

10 Attributes of the Motivated Coach

1) Clarity
Gives and receives accurate information.

2) Supportiveness
Committed to standing behind the class.

3) Confidence-builder
Develops a positive self-image for each student.

4) Mutuality
Strives to develop win-win relationships.

5) Perspective
Communicates the big picture.

6) Risk
Encourages risk-taking and rewards people for it.

7) Patience
Understands that long-term gain comes over time.

8) Excitement
Provides enthusiasm and inspiration.

9) Confidentiality
Places strong emphasis on trust.

10) Respect
Gives respect and receives it in return.

say or act like they don't. If they are making mistakes, pick up on that and counsel them through to success.

MENTOR THE STUDENTS WHO EXHIBIT AVERAGE PERFORMANCE.

Average performers need to be positively pushed to the next level of performance; to be challenged and shown the light. While the teacher should serve as the primary mentor, pairing the average performer with an above-average performer can also do wonders – for both parties. The protégé receives assistance and positive reinforcement from a talented peer, while the peer mentor becomes empowered to share his or her skills and knowledge. It also gives you more time to work with the below average performers, who usually need more guidance from an experienced educator, as they are less adept at learning new material on their own.

Research has shown that peer mentoring is one of the best ways to drive high performance among both middle and high performers in a business organization, and it's been wildly successful in Montessori schools, so why not adapt such a mentoring model to your classroom?

COACH THE STUDENTS WHO EXHIBIT ABOVE AVERAGE PERFORMANCE

One of the biggest mistakes that educators make is to assume that star students don't need any attention, encouragement or feedback, taking an "If it's not broken, don't fix it" approach with their best students, and instead, focusing all of their time and energy on improving the performance of struggling pupils.

Theory C practitioners, on the other hand, realize that

top performers are highly motivated and ambitious individuals who desire and even demand continuous challenges, mental stimulation and positive reinforcement. Nobody can continue running at full speed all the time without occasionally refueling and receiving a tune-up. Having their teacher serve as their coach provides top students with the encouragement, challenge and motivation to consistently achieve greatness.

As well as providing feedback, work with the top performers to set new goals, encouraging them to work on their own to learn above and beyond the constraints of class. This is part of the push-pull approach – working *with* them to push them harder and motivate them to do more than is expected of the average student.

RE-EVALUATE.

Students are in an ever-changing flux of performance. Below average performers become average performers, or better. Average performers become above average, or occasionally, show a dip in performance and drop down to below average. Above average students may plateau and become static. The effective Theory C teacher recognizes the importance of regularly evaluating performance changes and adapting his or her approach with each student. These teachers also look inward – examining what they may have done or not done whenever they see a drop in performance. The "C" in Theory C does not stand for "constant"; the classroom is a highly dynamic environment, and the top teachers keep their finger on the pulse of that environment, then take appropriate action.

Five Insights Top Teachers Possess

While each school and each classroom is unique, and every teacher must customize his or her class accordingly, there are several fundamental insights that the most successful educators share today:

1) People behave based on their thoughts.
Perception drives action; if a student thinks he is unintelligent, he will act unintelligently, but if he thinks he is valuable, competent, intelligent and creative, then he will accomplish remarkable things.

2) Individuality should be valued and explored.
By highlighting different beliefs, backgrounds and points of view, teachers present students with fresh new takes on old topics and challenge students to rethink ideas, possibilities and solutions.

3) Lack of motivation reflects discouragement.
If students lack enthusiasm and interest, it is highly likely that the teacher, albeit unwittingly, is teaching in a way that hinders students from feeling enthralled and engaged.

4) Consequences determine performance.
Classrooms where no acknowledgement or disciplinary action takes place (whenever such action is warranted) will invariably result in a loss of respect and control.

5) People treated responsibly will take on responsibility.
Give people a say in how to accomplish goals and objectives, and they are much more likely to give everything they've got to achieve those objectives. And in the event that they fall short of their target, empowered students are likely to take accountability for the lack of success and devise a new plan – or at least give a solid second effort – to meet their goal.

Key Points to Remember

- A **Theory C** teacher is one who acts as a coach, taking a customized, individualized approach to teaching while creating a positive classroom culture that fosters high levels of motivation and engagement.

- A coach's job is to mentor, motivate, train, plan for and communicate for his team.

- **Push-pull** your students: pushing them to work harder while pulling them alongside you.

- To be an effective Theory C teacher: assess current performance; counsel the students who exhibit below average performance; mentor the students who exhibit average performance; coach the students who exhibit above average performance; and re-evaluate.

A Story of Empowerment

To earn my undergraduate degree, I was required to take Calculus 1 and Calculus 2. To most people, this would not be a big deal. The only problem was that I had only taken Geometry and Pre-algebra in high school – falling way short on the prerequisite to tackle a monster like Calculus.

I showed up the first day of Calculus 1 leery of what I had gotten myself into, wondering if I would ever earn my degree. The course proved to be a challenge. The first go-around earned me the right to take the class again despite having worked very hard. The second time around, I managed to scrape by with a C, which earned me a ticket to Calculus 2 – the more advanced version of what I had just endured, with the addition of a little Algebra 2 just to spice it up some.

If I thought I was lost in Calculus 1, in Calculus 2, I was downright doomed. The first day of class, I walked in and took my seat towards the front. The teacher flew into the room, practically running, with a big smile on her face as she greeted her new students. She didn't even hesitate; before I could even grab a piece of paper, she started firing off questions and recapping the basics of Algebra 2. Her exact words were, "Let's start from the very basics, and work up from there." Students all around me had their hands up. They knew the answers. I realized that I was in way over my head.

Despite putting in countless hours of studying and spending hours working through homework assignments, I managed to remain clueless and lost throughout each Calculus 2 class. Then the day came for our first exam. Going into it, I thought there was a chance I could squeak by and pull off a miracle – maybe even a C. However, after turning in the exam, I had a different perspective – maybe with a "curve" I would end up with a passing grade.

*The following Tuesday rolled around, and I found myself back in my seat anxiously awaiting the exam results. My professor placed the sheet of paper in front of me face down and gave me a glaring look with a grin. I thought to myself, "Did I pull it off? Had I actually managed to scrape by?" I closed my eyes, turned the sheet over and found my numerical grade in the upper right hand corner of the page. Inscribed in red was an **11**. My heart sunk as I sat there lost and confused. How was I ever going to earn my degree if I couldn't pass this class? I had worked hard, hadn't missed a day of class and had turned in all of my homework. How could I have gotten an **11**?*

Right after class, I made my way to my Dean's office to get a withdrawal (drop-class) slip and rework my schedule. The Dean signed my drop slip and sent me on my way. I still needed my professor's signature to drop the class, so that evening I went down to the mathematics building and knocked on her door. After about three knocks, the door flung open and there she stood with a big smile, "How can I help you?"

I said, "I am here to drop your class."

She exclaimed, "You can't!"

I said, "Um, yes I can – I have a withdraw slip from the Dean's office and all you have to do is sign it."

*She refused. I reminded her that I was the student who got an **11** on the exam. She stepped back and said, "Oh!" then followed with, "You can't drop my class because I have not even begun to teach you. You need to come to class early and ask questions, you need to participate in class discussions, you need to get a tutor, you need to come down each night during my office hours to get help on your homework. You have to sleep, eat and love Calculus, and I am just the person to help you." I left her office thinking that this lady is absolutely crazy.*

The next scheduled class period, I was greeted with her familiar smile. She tore right into the lesson plan with enthusiasm and excitement. She then called on me to see if I understood what she was talking about. I sat in my chair shaking my head, completely lost and still wondering what I was doing in this class. Before I could finish wallowing in self-pity, I felt two hands grab the back of my shirt and pull me to the front of the class. The professor said, "If you don't get it, you have to get up and ask questions and come to the board and work through the problem until you get a solution."

I thought, "That's fine and dandy, but I'm the only student standing at the board working on problems."

As I finished the problem, she had the class clapping and cheering for me. I blushed profusely. She looked at me and said, "There, it's not so bad, is it? Now stand over here next to me because I know you'll have another question in just a minute." She then winked at me, smiled, and continued her lesson at an

41

ever-alarming pace.

Let's just say that my place from then on was at the chalk-board in front of the class. The second exam came along, and this time I didn't have any expectations. I went into the test knowing I had given it my all and that if I failed again, it just wasn't meant to be. I took the test and left the class knowing that I had done really well. There were numerous problems that I had seen before and worked out with my tutor. I couldn't wait to see my grade.

The day the exam was to be returned, I was sitting in my chair feeling anxious and saying to myself, "If I get less than a C, I'm leaving immediately. There is no reason to fight this thing only to have to come back and do it again next semester."

My professor placed my exam down on my desk with a smile and a few chuckles and said, "I told you math was fun and that you would love this class." I turned my exam over and saw an __82__ written in red ink at the upper right hand corner of the page.

"Are you kidding me?!" I shouted internally. It was one of the greatest days I ever had in college. I knew I was going to pass Calculus 2 despite only having taken Pre-algebra and Geometry in high school.

The rest of the semester I kept at it, working hard and giving it my all. Then came time for the final exam, which counted for 50% of our final grade. I approached this test with the same focus and intensity as a football player in the Super Bowl. I visited my professor often, went to tutoring every day and studied with another student who had an A in the class.

I went into the exam knowing that I had left nothing on the table. I was eager to hear the whistle blow. There were 500 students packed into the auditorium, and I was sitting in the very back, up high, with a bunch of students I had never seen before. Before I knew it, my test was in front of me, and I dug in.

I could hear the other 499 pencils scratching numbers on paper, and an occasional eraser and sigh of frustration.

When I finished, I threw my head back, set my pencil down on my desk and let out a chuckle with my eyes closed. When I opened them, 499 students were looking at me in utter amazement. I grabbed my paper and backpack and started making my way down to the stage where my professor was sitting. My peers were looking at me like I was the smartest student around. The students and I weren't the only ones shocked that I had finished the exam first; my professor had a look of astonishment. As I got closer to the front of the stage, she put her pen down and focused on me completely. I walked up the four steps to the stage, set my exam down in front of her and just smiled. She looked at me and asked, "How did you do?"

I said, "I've never seen this stuff before in my life," then turned around and started making my way back down the stage, out of the auditorium and home for a well rested summer – knowing that I was going to have take this class again and probably end up with the same crazy lady as my professor.

I got only about two steps down when she shouted to me, "Bryan, you are horrible in math." I thought, "Thanks. Thanks for building my self-esteem, especially after I have worked my tail off all semester long." Then she continued: "But your work ethic and dedication are remarkable. It made me feel good to have a student like you try so hard. With that type of dedication, you are going to be a success." She then gave me a double thumbs-up. Even more importantly, she gave me a C in the class.

My professor had counseled and mentored and coached me the entire semester. She was passionate and enthusiastic about math; she pushed and pulled me through the process, taking me as far as I could go in math. And although it was not very far, she sparked something in me. That is what a student-centric, motivated, Theory C teacher does – inspires the student to want to learn. You can't just tell a student to get motivated

43

and expect results. A student first has to become inspired, and **then** *the inspiration brings forth motivation, resulting in enthusiasm, which in turn, makes the student have an impact. Your job as an educator is to inspire!*

SECTION II
Teacher as Coach: Mentor, Motivator, Communicator

Force, by definition, is met with resistance. A Zen master never forces his students to learn: he simply guides them through the paths they're already on.

Chapter 3
Someone to Look Up To

Closing the Gap

Although the role of the coach was briefly defined in Chapter 2, there is still a gap for the majority of teachers, who have spent their careers teaching, instead of coaching. "Okay," you might ask, "my job is to be a coach … I'm supposed to mentor my students and motivate them … how on *earth* do I *do* that?"

I'm glad you asked. Later on we'll go into more detail regarding the "doing" of a Theory C teacher – developing lesson plans, edutaining your students and so on. But first we have to learn the "being" – how to be a mentor, how to be a motivator and how to be an effective

47

communicator. These are the foundations of a coach; if you can't inspire your athletes, it doesn't matter how good your game plan is, you won't win games.

So, let's start with the mentor.

Throughout literature, both ancient and contemporary, one of the most predominant elements – second only to the hero himself – is the mentor. The mentor isn't always a main character – in fact, he often appears in only a few scenes – but he's always there, because someone needs to inspire the hero into action.

So, let's begin by looking at some of the greatest mentors in history:

Merlin, Morpheus & Obi-Wan Kenobe

Merlin was a great magician, who served as mentor to King Arthur in the Arthurian legend. Morpheus, in *The Matrix*, is Captain of the Nebuchadnezzar, and the person who finds Neo and introduces him to the real world. And Obi-Wan, of course, is the great Jedi knight who teaches Luke Skywalker the ways of the Force in *Star Wars*.

These three people or characters provide excellent examples of what it is to be a mentor to a young student, and outlined below is their function within each story.

Rescue from Without

The mentor's first job is always to rescue the hero from some external threat. In Arthurian legend, Arthur finds Merlin's house while he's lost in the woods. In *The Matrix*, Morpheus attempts to help Neo escape from the agents, and then he successfully removes the tracking device the agents have implanted in Neo's belly. And Obi-Wan first appears to frighten away the Sand People.

The threats to your students may not be as imminent as Agent Smith or the Sand People, but they are no less real: a culture of negativity, drugs, violence, teen pregnancies, parents who don't take an interest in their children's education, parents who spoil their children, over-reliance on technological communication, which hampers face-to-face interaction ... all of these pose a threat to a student's ability to grow and develop into a mature, successful adult.

The degree of imminence will dictate how much of a rescue is required. A 12-year-old using drugs requires a different course of action than a parent spoiling his child. In fact, the latter doesn't necessarily require any direct course of action on your part at all. But as a Theory C teacher, you should start by recognizing what each individual student is struggling with or running from, and take it upon yourself to provide an opportunity for your student to escape from that struggle.

Providing the Key to the Hero's Identity

The next role of the mentor is to provide the hero with key information that he needs in order to know who he is: Arthur's real father was the King of England, Neo was "The One," and Luke's father was a great Jedi knight who was killed by Darth Vader.

The latter is particularly interesting: Luke had known of the strange hermit "Old Ben Kenobe" his entire life, but only later found out that Ben knew his father. Prior to the revelation of this information, Luke was not a hero, he was simply a farm-boy (and a whiny one at that). It was

49

only in the discovery of his true identity that he would have the motivation to leap into the scary world of the unknown.

Your job in mentoring your students is to provide them with the key information they need *about themselves* in order to complete their journey as successful adults. What are their strengths that will guide them toward success? What are their weaknesses, which must be developed along the way? What can you say that will inspire them to learn; that is, to make the choice to take on *their* journey?

Obviously, in most cases, you won't know your students as well as Merlin, who sees the future, Morpheus, who has consummate surveillance capabilities, or Obi-Wan, who has been watching over Luke his entire life. So for you, providing your students with the keys to their identity will take a concentrated effort once you meet them.

Successful teachers are the ones who take the time to get to know their students. So take the time, early on in class, to have one-on-one meetings, to have your students complete surveys, or to otherwise do what it takes to learn the dreams and goals of the people you're teaching. Students want to know that you care, and if you show this up front, You'll have a much easier time convincing them that you're interested in *them* later on when they start to struggle or run into conflict.

A Former Hero

The mentor is always someone who is battle-tested – he has gone on his own journey, he has been his own hero in the past, and he is simply at the endpoint of his own character arc, where his job is to inspire the hero to take on a great journey of his own. Merlin can only be Arthur's mentor because he himself had been on a great many adventures, and Obi-Wan was a great Jedi knight himself.

Though the mentor is older than the hero, it is not his age that stops him from being the hero of this particular tale – rather, it is a matter of destiny. Morpheus is a great officer, but it is not his role to end the war against the machines; it is Neo's. Obi-Wan is a great Jedi, but it is not his role to bring balance to the Force.

You are a great adult. You have followed your own path to greatness, and it has led you exactly where you need to be, to your destiny of coaching and mentoring young minds. Your role, then, is to inspire these students – through tales and anecdotes from your own life experience – to pursue their destiny, whatever that may be.

The point is to **be open to sharing your own life with your students**, so that they can see that you're not just some schmuck who has authority over them this year. Show them that you're a real human being with successes and failures. This display of truth is a demonstration of respect for them, and it will inspire them to respect you and follow in your footsteps.

PREMATURE DEATH

Obi-Wan dies right before Luke needs him the most. Morpheus is captured and rendered unable to help Neo in his development. Merlin is seduced by the Lady of the Lake, who casts him into the land of fairy keeping.

Don't worry, though. Remarkably, in each of these

deaths the mentor doesn't actually die. Even in stories where the mentor physically dies, he is in some way re-born or immortalized in a way that makes him even more powerful. Obi-Wan, for example, lets himself be killed by Darth Vader so that he can be embedded in Luke's psyche, no longer confined to the physical realm. In *The Lord of the Rings: The Fellowship of the Ring*, Gandalf the Grey plummets to his death, only to come back in the next installment as Gandalf the White. In *The Lion, the Witch & the Wardrobe*, Aslan sacrifices himself and is reborn because "when a willing victim who had committed no treachery was killed in a traitor's stead, the Table would crack and Death itself would start working backward."

The reason these mentors never actually died was because, as an allegory for life, the death simply represented the final step of his character arc: the journey from mentor to legend. By taking this step, he immortalizes himself and simultaneously forces the hero to win the final battle on his own, which is the most critical step of the hero's journey.

So you don't have to die to successfully mentor your students. (Whew!) But you *do* have to *metaphorically* kill yourself off. *At times, you need to walk away and let them do it on their own.* Only then will they develop the skills and the confidence they require to successfully complete their journey. And feel free to come back later and let them know that it was all just part of their training – great mentors always do.

And when you do come back, you achieve the status of legend.

Cleaning the Fish Tank

In practical application, the most important aspect of being a mentor is setting a positive example. This means being an inspired, motivated teacher.

Whoever says, "Do as I say, not as I do," is both saying and doing something very stupid.

Imagine you're a fish swimming around in a gigantic tank filled with clear blue water. And you're excited! Every day you wake up, looking forward to swimming and teaching every guppy in the tank that he can be a superstar. Yippee!!

But then, one day, the Fish Principal says, "You can't tell every guppy that he'll grow up to be a superstar. Most of them won't, and you're just setting up false expectations that will disappoint them in life." You don't like hearing this, so you poop in your fish tank.

But there's still plenty of clear blue water, so you continue swimming around, telling all the guppies to follow their dreams! They can make their dreams come true!

Healthy Eating: The Secret Ingredient to Building Enthusiasm

I cannot stress enough how vitally important diet is to maintaining high levels of energy and enthusiasm. You are, indeed, what you eat. Too many teachers eat a heavy lunch high in fat, sodium and/or sugar, then return to the classroom and spend the rest of the day trying to keep their eyes open.

Ideally, you should eat a well-balanced, substantial breakfast and a moderate lunch and dinner high in lean protein (chicken/turkey breast, fish, lean beef/pork), smart carbs (whole- or multi-grains) and fresh vegetables. In between meals, enjoy a couple of healthy snacks (fresh fruit, yogurt, energy bars). If you eat reasonable portions five or six times a day, your energy level will increase because your metabolism will work at a steady rate.

And then the Tank Administrator tells you that you have to teach the guppies to pass their swimming exam at the end of the year, or you don't get a raise. Again, you poop in the tank.

Over time, what was once clear blue water is murky and brown, and instead of swimming excitedly you're mulching through the murk. But you don't really notice it, because all the other fish your age are doing the same thing.

Then you realize that you just made all that poop yourself. Yes, there are bossy fish out there and there are restrictions within the tank, but *you're* the one who made the water nasty to swim in. So you realize, it's time to clean you're tank! One by one, you take each little fish poop and throw it out of the tank, and before you know it, there you are again, still restricted by the walls of the tank, but now inspired to teach guppies to make their dreams come true.

It's a silly analogy, maybe, but its implication is enormous. Over time, teachers who were once inspired lose sight of the reason they entered the education industry to begin with, and it becomes just a job.

Ask yourself the following questions: Do you look forward to going to work? When you leave, are you happy you were there? Do you laugh or smile frequently? Can you see the difference you make?

Now, ask yourself: Do you feel like you don't have enough time in the day? Do you walk around staring at the floor? Has your energy level decreased? Does your life lack adventure or direction? Have you become more introverted? Do you have the experience of frequent or constant anxiety, pressure or loss of control? Have eating habits changed or use of alcohol, tobacco or drugs (both legal and illegal) increased?

Obviously, you want to be answering "yes" to the first set of questions and "no" to the second set. If you find yourself on the wrong side of these questions, it's time to take action and choose the path to enthusiasm.

EXIT YOUR COMFORT ZONE

Motivation starts by being inspired. Once you're inspired, you become motivated, and then enthusiastic, which leads to becoming influential and contagious.

Unfortunately, we humans are creatures of habit, creating routines and schedules that we adhere to in an attempt to feel as if we have some sense of control and order in our lives. This keeps us trapped in our "comfort" zone, often deadening our senses and resulting in an uninspired – or worse, dismal – outlook on life. Therein lies the irony: too much time in the comfort zone results in ample psychological and emotional discomfort.

Taking on new challenges taxes your creativity, sharpens your instincts and provides a platform for increased knowledge and inspiration. New experiences tap into the superpowers that are tucked away in your subconscious brain. Whether you pursue a new hobby or activity, continue your formal education, or volunteer your time for a worthy cause, challenging yourself every day makes your life and work more meaningful. And you need to find life and work meaningful to feel motivated and to have any chance of fostering high levels of motivation in others.

While not easy, it's critical to force yourself out of a complacent, apathetic state to give yourself a chance to become more inspired.

> *Inspiration sometimes leads to action.*
> *Action __always__ leads to inspiration.*

Write down one new adventure you will undertake this year. Write down three things you can do differently. Ask people what they know you would never do, and then do it.

The important thing is to break the routine, just to break the monotony. It's a sometimes small, but often important, step toward inspiration.

GIVE THANKS

Every night before you fall asleep, find two or three things to be thankful for. This will ultimately lead to gratitude for the opportunity to participate in the wonder of life and will leave you looking forward to tomorrow, anticipating another opportunity to sip the nectar of life.

Then, each morning when you awaken, have a little pep-talk with yourself. Acknowledge all the wonderful things in your life. Reflect for a moment on those things you cherish most. Be thankful that today is another day of "vacation." Create a goal to accomplish or lesson to learn for the day. Avoid thinking about the problems or obligations facing you today; by maintaining a high level of enthusiasm, these tasks can be easily managed.

Ultimately, your attitude for the day begins long

before you step into the classroom, so focus on starting the day on a positive note.

Problems Worth Having

In life, there are problems, and problems are unavoidable. This is a fact. Consider that every solution, itself, poses a problem. For example, in the late 19th century, there was a terrible problem with pollution in the United States; it was caused by horse manure in the streets. Then, there was this amazing invention – the automobile – which everyone immediately saw would reduce the need for horses in the streets, thus putting an end to pollution!

Some more examples: You didn't want to live at home, so you moved out when you were 18. Rent? Parents calling you all the time, mad that you don't call them? No problem! Or you didn't want to be single, so you got married. Poof, all your problems disappeared!

So, given that your life is going to have problems, you might as well create problems worthy of your life. Martin Luther King, Jr. decided that his problem was that America's black and white citizens were not treated as equals. Muhatma Gandhi decided his problem was that the British continued to occupy India. These were problems worth having, and in the context of these problems, "Who put chalk in the eraser?" sort of becomes a non-issue.

If you're a teacher, you probably already have a problem worth having: shaping young minds to be the best they can be. But it helps to think about your obstacles in this way, putting them in perspective and giving you the choice to tackle the ones that are most important to you.

"I AM" PRINCIPLE

You have a conscious and a subconscious part of your mind. Some call it the internal (subconscious) and external (conscious). Your subconscious serves as the computer system that takes and processes information from the conscious. What you consciously think is believed by your subconscious, which in turn, goes to work and turns the thought into a reality. For example, if a teacher constantly says to him- or herself something like, "I don't want a bunch of students in my class who are disruptive and not interested in what I'm teaching," then amazingly, those are the exact type of students the teacher will end up having. Saying and thinking things like, "These kids today are just rude and don't want to learn" impregnates your subconscious, and helps turn negative thoughts into reality. What you think is what you get.

So the bottom line is, whenever you want to alter your behavior and attitudes, convince yourself that you're already that way. If you feel yourself slowing, tell yourself, "I am an unstoppable energy machine ready for action." No matter what characteristic you wish to develop, picture yourself the way you want to be and declare it. Repeat the affirmation until you believe it. Eventually, you will enhance your self-esteem and positively influence everyone you encounter.

MEET NEW PEOPLE

Whether at school, work-related functions/events or social gatherings, every day you interact with people – some familiar, others for the first time. Most of the people you encounter are merely acquaintances, but you can choose, if you wish, to create more meaningful friendships by getting to know selected people on a more personal level. Such relationships serve to enhance your morale and connection to people, as well as help expand your knowledge and viewpoints (if you listen and remain open to the ideas, opinions and experiences of others).

Creating new friendships also helps to develop your "positive optimistic personality." In other words, when you're getting to know someone, you are usually on your best behavior. As you go through the process of fostering a friendship with them, conversations will be naturally more focused on positive issues, thus generating more positive energy and enthusiasm.

The man who believes he can do something is probably right, and so is the man who believes he can't.

MISSION & VALUES

Values are principles, standards or qualities that are considered worthwhile or desirable. Well-defined values will help you build a strong foundation upon which you can build a more meaningful life. In other words, values are your self-worth; your beliefs and the manner in which you choose to represent yourself will determine how others see you.

When was the last time you asked yourself what you stand for or what factors or attributes make you who you are? The next time you're chatting with a friend, ask him or her that question; few people can answer it effortlessly. But if you think about what makes you a great person, you can create – and write down – your values and how they impact your behavioral patterns, which is the path to being the best person you can be.

To start, it helps to create your very own mission statement, a paragraph that defines your life purpose – how you aim to live your life and the type of person you strive to be.

Every person is born with a mission; it is your job in life to discover it.

This process begins simply by starting to think about it. The moment you begin to think and write about your mission, your brain will begin to search deep inside of you. You may not know your purpose today, tomorrow or even a year or two from now, but thinking about it is part of the discovery. These next few exercises will help.

On a piece of paper, write down your answers to the following questions:

▶ How would you like to be remembered?
▶ What have you always dreamed of contributing to the world?
▶ When people think of you, what might they say are your most outstanding characteristics?
▶ What do you really want from your life?
▶ What are some principles by which you live your life?

Take a few moments to look back over your answers. What you wrote down is what you're all about. Based on this information, take some time now and develop a mission statement and a list of your five most important values and what they mean to you.

From this day forward, consider your mission statement and your values before taking action or making critical and consequential decisions. Embracing and committing to a noble set of values will not only help you earn the respect and trust of others, it establishes strong self-worth and self-confidence – attributes that fuel enthusiasm and motivation; attributes that make you positively infectious.

> *The difference between ordinary and extraordinary is a little extra.*

Key Points to Remember

• *As a mentor, your job is to "rescue" your disciples from external threats, provide information that will help them in their journey, share with them your exploits as a former hero and "kill yourself off" so they learn to succeed on their own.*

• *You must also, as a mentor, show enthusiasm yourself. If you find yourself lacking in enthusiasm, exit your comfort zone, give thanks for the wonder of life, create problems worth having, convince yourself that you already are the way you want to be, meet new people and/or create a mission and values statement.*

• *Every person is born with a mission; it is your job in life to discover it.*

Chapter 4
Communication: The Fiese Method to Group Dynamics

There's a lot of information in this chapter that pertains not just to teaching, but to life in general. But there is something more here, which relates directly to teaching, and that's the *Fiese Method to Group Dynamics*. Throughout the chapter, you'll get a great deal of information about *how* human beings communicate. The

Fiese Method to Group Dynamics is basically just a fancy way of saying that effective communication as a Gen-Next teacher requires moving beyond *your* innate/dominant ways of communicating and instead incorporating all the ways people communicate. That way they *all* get it – not just the ones who communicate in the same way you do.

We'll get into the ways people communicate in a minute. For now, let's start with the basics.

LISTENING

A few facts about listening:

• Studies have shown that 40% of an entry-level person's salary is actually pay for listening. Studies have also proven that leaders are paid 80% of their salary to listen. Good listeners make good friends, teachers, leaders, parents and spouses. Unfortunately, as a society, we listen with 33% of our true capacity – and that is decreasing rapidly.

• When you are talking with someone, only 7% of what is communicated comes from your words. They get the rest of your message via your tone of voice (38%) and body language (55%). While communicating, we go

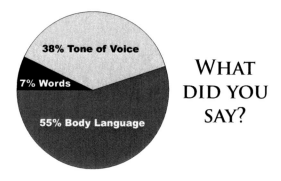

through what is called an encode/decode process. As a person speaks, they are encoding a message with words and delivering it with tone and body language. The receiver decodes the message, which goes through his own filtering system and he then assigns meaning, relevance and importance to the words.

• A person can only listen for about 15 seconds (two to three sentences) before they go into "la-la land." The decoder is always two seconds behind the encoder, thus after 15 seconds, the former ponders the new information and then decides if they want to go back and listen.

There are two important points to take from these facts. First, nearly 80% of a teacher's time should be spent with open ears and an open mind, taking in what students are saying, and doing and allowing such information to help shape the class and engage students in the learning process. What? That can't be right! *Eighty percen*t of your time in class should be spent listening? We'll get to this in more detail in Chapter 6, but for now, consider the difference between a class that's being lectured at and one in which the students are actively involved, debating each other and coming up with their own solutions, while you are acting simply as the moderator. I know which class I'd rather be in.

Nothing kills communication like the illusion that it has already been accomplished.

The second important point to take from these facts about listening is that your students will only believe you if you believe yourself. For example, imagine it's the first

65

day of school, and you get up in front of the class and say, "Good morning. I am really excited to have each of you in my class. This will be a fun and exciting year." If you say such things with no expression and no enthusiasm, the students will not believe you're excited or that it's going to be a fun year. However, if you utter your welcoming sentiments with a smile and a bubbly tone of voice, along with some emotive hand gestures, you will be more believable and students more engaged and excited to commence the new school year with you.

ACTIVE & REFLECTIVE LISTENING

Active listening describes the physical use of body language to communicate that you are paying attention, while *reflective listening* refers to the mental concentration that allows you to absorb what the speaker is saying. Both are important for effective communication. Imagine if you're at a party, and someone walks up to you, shakes your hand, looks you in the eye and tells you his name, and the only thing you can think about is his crazy hairdo. Now imagine, at that same party, you introduce yourself to someone who's looking over your shoulder at something that's going on behind you. In both instances, only one form of listening is being used, and neither will result in satisfactory interactions.

To translate this to the classroom, there's a very simple, three-step process to engage your students to move closer to 80% listening:

Step 1: Ask a pointed question.
"Where is the capital of the United States?"

Step 2: Ask an open-ended question.
"Why is it there?"

Step 3: Ask a reflective question.

"So they decided to put the nation's capital on the Potomac, which was the border between the Northern and Southern states ... why would they do that? Was it a good idea? ... etc."

By asking questions in this way, both you and the students will be listening and actively engaged in the conversation.

NEURO-LINGUISTIC PROGRAMMING (NLP)

Being a Theory C teacher requires customizing your communication to each individual student, and that starts with connecting to the students' verbal patterns. Here's where we start to get into the different "ways of communicating" mentioned at the top of this chapter.

Don't be too afraid of the hairy hyphenated term in the subhead of this section. It may seem scary, but the idea behind it is relatively straightforward (besides, we've assigned it a nice, neat acronym – NLP – to reduce the intimidation factor).

FAST FACT

In general, females are better than males with regard to eye contact. If you watch five year-old boys and 50 year-old men, you will notice they do the exact same thing. In a conversation, they will look left, right, down, and up, and when their eyes connect with the other person's, they immediately look away. It is an innate behavior.

Developed in 1975 by Richard Bandler and John Grinder, NLP identifies the ways in which we have been "programmed" to think, act and feel. It is, in essence, the science of how the brain codes learning and experience. This coding affects all communication and behavior. It affects how we learn and how we experience the world around us. Our perceptions of the world are directly related to

67

the senses: audio, visual and kinesthetic.

NLP is extremely useful in education, as it is a powerful tool for student empowerment. We've already said that your job as a coach is to tap the unique characteristics of each student and help them reach their full potential, and with an understanding of NLP you can study the verbal and nonverbal language of every child to identify how each one communicates – and therefore learns – best.

The core of NLP is modeling: Learning to replicate the excellence of someone highly proficient in a desirable skill in a way that allows us learn and to teach that ability quickly and efficiently. And that's what Bandler and Grinder did with the communication skills of philosophers Erickson and Jean-Paul Sartre, who studied the subconscious behaviors of humans. Bandler and Grindler built a model of Erickson's and Satre's skills, beliefs and attitudes that make it easier for anyone to learn to use words and nonverbal communications more effectively and with greater precision. It's within these skills and attitudes that the magic of NLP resides, both for personal change and for more effective communications skills.

MODALITIES

In a large part, NLP is about noticing patterns. The first step is to pay attention to the process of your interaction with others. Bandler and Grinder discovered that by looking at someone's eyes, you could tell how they think as opposed to what they think. You can tell what's going on "inside." You uncover what are called "modalities." In a nutshell, a modality is a model for what people do in their heads as they make sense of the world.

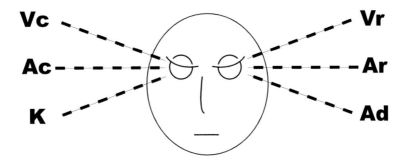

There are six major modalities, as represented in the figure above. (Note: The figure represents the six modalities for a "normal" right-handed person. Many left-handed people and some ambidextrous people will have eye movements that are reversed.) Based on observations by Bandler and Grinder, when people look up, they're visualizing. When they look horizontally to the left and right, they're either remembering or constructing sounds. When they look downward and to their right, they're accessing their feelings. And when they look downward and to their left, they're talking to themselves (Auditory Digital).

Let's take a closer look at each of the six modalities represented in the figure:

Vr - Visual Remembered (Visual Recall) – *Seeing images from memory; recalling things you have seen before.* Some questions that trigger the Vr modality include: "What color was the room you grew up in?" "What color is your car?" and "What did the suspect look like?"

Vc - Visual Constructed (Visual Created) – *Seeing images in your head of things that you have never seen before.* Whenever you are making things up, you are using Visual Constructed. A question that could trigger the Vc modality is: "What would your house look like if it were painted red?"

Ar - Auditory Remembered (Auditory Recall) – *Remembering sounds or voices that you've heard before or things that you've said to yourself before.* When you ask someone, "What was the very last thing I said?" you'll notice that they typically will look in the direction indicated in the above figure while thinking. Another question that would trigger the Ar modality is "Can you remember your grandmother's voice?"

Ac - Auditory Constructed (Auditory Created) – *Making up sounds that you've not heard before.* Possible trigger question: "What would I sound like if I had a deep raspy voice?"

K - Kinesthetic (Feelings, Sense of Touch) – *Accessing your feelings.* Possible trigger question: "How do you feel about laying out at the beach?"

Ad - Auditory Digital (Talking to Yourself) – *Having internal dialogue.* Possible trigger question: "Can I recite the Pledge of Allegiance?"

As you can see, every time we access our brain, we typically move our eyes in a particular direction that facilitates the use of a certain part of our neurology. The mind and body are absolutely interconnected.

REPRESENTATIONAL SYSTEMS DEFINED

Each individual tends to depend on one representational system (Visual, Auditory or Kinesthetic) more than another as we access information and use it to make sense out of the world around us.

Imagine checking into a hotel where the clerk tells you that your room is around the corner, down the hall, past the vending machine, turn right, up the elevator to the third floor, right through the double doors, follow the hall

EYES: WINDOW TO YOUR CLASSROOM

Mastering the art of effective eye contact is critical for captivating and connecting with a classroom and for "reading" (that is, listening to) your students' body language.

Tips for effectively communicating with your eyes:

1. *Always maintain eye contact whenever possible, even (and especially) during presentations with slides, etc.*

2. *Visually break the classroom up into manageable clusters and "work" each section equally. In large groups, make eye contact with one person in a cluster and then move on – peripheral vision will take care of the rest.*

3. *Adopt a random pattern. That is, avoid the tendency to "ping-pong" back and forth with your eyes.*

4. *Look at and speak to the opposite side of the room from where you are standing, as shown in this diagram. Your presence and proximity already creates a sense of intimacy with the people physically closest to you.*

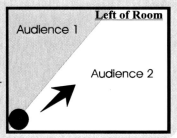

71

around to the right and the room is on the left. If you're an auditory person you would no doubt say thank you, having processed it all, and march on your merry way. A visual learner will have a look of utter confusion, so the clerk pulls out a map and highlighter and shows it to you. You take the map as a reference guide, and all is right with the world. But a kinesthetic learner will still have no idea, and will need to be taken there, or at least pointed

Audio	Visual	Kinesthetic
Buzz	Look	Support
Ring	Picture	Attack
Noisy	See	Warm
Sound	Show	Cold
Echo	Horizon	Electric
Hear	Hazy	Tickle
Say	Dull	Play
Tone	Brilliant	Vibes
Listen	Inspect	Dig
Talk	Scan	Press
Bell	Foggy	Rough
Call	Vague	Grasp
Whine	Diagram	Balance
Clang	Hide	Fumble

in the right direction with the instruction to follow the signs. But once the kinesthetic learner has been there once, he'll have no problem finding that hotel room time and time again, while the auditory learner will have to think back and remember the oral instructions to find his way back.

Let's go over the major characteristics of each mode:

Visual – Typically, people who are in a visual mode stand, or sit, with their heads and/or bodies erect with their eyes up and breathe from the top of their lungs. They often sit forward in the chair or on the edge of the chair. They tend to be more organized, neat, well groomed and orderly; more deliberate; more appearance oriented and sometimes quieter. Visual people are good spellers. They memorize by seeing pictures and are less distracted by noise. They often have trouble remembering verbal instructions and are bored by long verbal explanations because their minds tend to wander. They would rather read than be read to. Visual people will be interested in how someone looks at them and will respond to being taken places and being bought things. They will tend to use words like: See, Look, Focus, Watch, Seems, Appear.

Auditory – People with an auditory tendency will breathe from the middle of the chest, typically talk to themselves and are easily distracted by noise. They may find math and writing more difficult than spoken language. They like music and learn by listening. They memorize by steps, procedures and sequence. An auditory person is often interested in being told how they're doing, and responds to a certain set of words or tone of voice. They tend to use words and phrases like: Listen, Talk, Say, Speak, Hear, Sounds like ….

Kinesthetic – Kinesthetic people typically breathe from the bottom of their lungs, so you'll see their stomach go in and out as they breathe. Their posture is often more slumped over, and they often move and talk very slowly. They will generally access their feelings and emotions to "get a feel" for what they're doing. They respond to physical rewards and touching. They also stand close to people and touch them. They are often physically coordinated people (athletes) and may move around a lot. They memorize by doing or by walking through something. They use words like: Feel, Touch, Hold, Grasp, Handle.

Good communicators will adapt to the others person's verbal pattern without thought!

The chart on the previous page provides some understanding of the words people tend to use if they are auditory, visual or kinesthetic.

Six Brain Functions

To take NLP one step further, there are six brain functions that dictate how a person learns. Evaluate each person in your classroom and determine if he or she is a/an:

1. **Authoritative student**
2. **Deductive student**
3. **Emotional student**
4. **Intuitive student**
5. **Sensory experience student**
6. **Test-driver student**

Authoritative students are task-oriented and pride themselves on doing exactly what is asked of them, and no more. They like structure, but lack vision, and seek guidance from others rather than taking initiative.

Deductive logic students are analytical. They demand facts, figures and data when making decisions. They take a scientific approach to a lesson.

Emotional students have the need to be involved and to socialize. These students like to work in groups and crave attention and group interaction. They are likely the students in the class who like to talk with friends and discuss the lesson.

Intuitive students act on a hunch. They listen to their internal voice when making decisions. For example: Let's say an intuitive student comes to you and asks for advice. You provide an answer, then two weeks later they come back with the same question. You provide them the same answer, and they ponder it for a while. It's not that they're not taking your advice; rather they're waiting for something inside of them to tell them it is the right decision. They may say something like, it "doesn't feel right".

Sensory experience students use all their senses to process information and learn. For example: If you are teaching sensory children a new software program, they will want to work through the program as you're explaining it to them. They want to see it, hear it, feel it, etc.

Test driver students demand to know what the end result is going to be before starting an assignment. They are goal-oriented, visual students – they want to know exactly what the journey from Point A to Point B is going to be like.

To show a more concrete example of the differences between these brain functions, imagine you're putting together a swing set. A test driver will take all the pieces out, lean the box against the fence with the picture clearly displayed and use the picture as a means of putting together the swing set. They won't look at the manual, just the picture. The sensory experience person lays all the pieces out and begins assembling the set. If they get stuck they might look through the manual, but once they get frustrated, they'll just start jamming the pieces together until it fits. An intuitive person will get stuck, walk away, think about it over lunch, and when the answer comes to them, they will go back and fix the problem. It could take months to complete the project. The emotional person will invite friends over for pizza and work on it as a group. The analytical mind will thoroughly read through the manual, criticize much of the design, and if possible, engineer new parts. Finally, the authoritative person, when stuck, will call the 1-800 hotline to get help, and keep them on the line as long as possible.

So you're a teacher facilitating learning in an environment where the students have all these different brain functions, you might start by asking questions, giving out the assignment, making sure the students know what the end goal is and asking them questions based on their modalities.

Personal Communication Styles

As with modalities, it's important to understand each student's personal communication style in order to better connect with students on an individual basis, and thus, enhance your ability to inspire and empower.

Personal communication styles are based on two dimensions of behavior: 1) Direct vs. Indirect; and 2) Supporting vs. Controlling. Some people are Direct and Controlling, others Indirect and Supporting; some are Direct and Supporting, others Indirect and Controlling.

The two charts on the following pages are a concise synopsis of the components of each of the two dimensions. Think of your own students and categorize generally – not forcefully pigeon-hole – each student based on the following:

DIRECT VS. INDIRECT

	DIRECT	INDIRECT
Pace	*Fast-paced, assertive, tendency to take charge.*	*Slow-paced, low-key, often even meek.*
Risk	*Confront change, risk and decision-making head on.*	*Cautious in approach to risk, decision-making and change.*
Assertiveness	*Outspoken, often dominate conversations and classroom discussions. Quick to argue a point.*	*Tentative to contribute to discussions. Often qualify suggestions with phrases like, "This is just an idea ... " or "I'm not sure if this makes sense ..."*
Competitiveness	*Competitive, impatient and confrontational; thrive on accomplishments.*	*Avoid conflict; diplomatic, patient and cooperative; will only stand their ground with strong convictions about an issue.*
Confidence	*Loud, confident, maintain strong eye contact, and have a firm handshake.*	*Quieter, slower, reserved and less confident, with a gentle handshake.*
Rules	*"It's easier to beg forgiveness than ask permission."*	*Seeks approval before acting.*
Visual Appearance	*Bold.*	*Conservative.*

Supporting vs. Controlling

	Supporting	Controlling
Emotions	Open; animated facial expressions and physical gestures.	Reserved; often called "poker faces."
Self-expression	Comfortable expressing joy, sadness and other emotions quickly and unabashedly to almost anyone.	More physically, mentally and emotionally closed. Seldom rowdy.
Personal Space	Maintain closer physical proximity; tend to be huggers, hand shakers and touchers.	Avoid physical contact; refer to stay a safe distance from others.
Relationships	Informal; prefer relaxed, warm relationships.	Prefer working alone; put little value on opinions and feelings.
Conversation	Enjoy loose, amusing conversations; frequently tell stories and anecdotes, often about personal embarrassing incidents.	Task-oriented; dislike digression from their agendas. More comfortable operating in an intelligent mode
Time Management	Prefer unstructured time and are seldom disturbed when other people waste their time.	Champions of time management; efficiency experts.
Decision-making	Feeling-oriented decision makers. Value their hunches and the feelings of others.	Fact-oriented decision makers; need to see statistics and other hard evidence.

THE FIESE METHOD TO GROUP DYNAMICS

Now that we've given you all this information, you may be wondering how to use it. This is where the Fiese Method to Group Dynamics comes in.

Oakland A's general manager Billy Beane once said that good players make lousy coaches, because they want you to do everything the same way they did it. Bad players don't have that problem: they don't care how you do it, as long as you do it better.

Similarly, in communication, the natural tendency of a teacher is to default to his or her dominant communication modes. "Be quiet!" is the shout of a teacher with an auditory modality. Math teachers, more often than not, are deductive in their brain function and will try to use logic, logic, logic when teaching their students. And professors who do nothing but lecture, day-in, day-out, are more often than not indirect communicators.

The Fiese Method to Group Dynamics is to incorporate all these types of communication in class, so that all your students get it.

When teaching a lesson, make sure to use all three representational modes: *explain* the subject matter, *show* with a presentation or visual examples and *assign* the students practice work so they can do it themselves. Look for opportunities, in every class, to incorporate logic, group interaction, intuition and tangible goals. Look for ways to get the passive people involved. Put the supporters and controllers together in a way that will give them time to freely explore but toward a fact-based result.

Keys to Communication: Avoid F.A.I.L.U.R.E.

Fear
Causes irrational thoughts and behavior, closing off communication.

Assumptions
Often result in conflict and/or in passing judgment too soon.

Insensitivity
Is an old-school approach to teaching; Gen-Nexters need you to pay attention to their emotions.

Labeling
Is contagious and alienates students into thinking the teacher never gave them a chance.

Uncertainty
Leads to anxiety and fear, so be clear when giving instructions.

Resentment
Kills open communication, so rebuild trust whenever it is damaged.

Ego
Is not the same as confidence; students don't listen to teachers who are arrogant or egotistical.

Most of you are probably already doing some of the above, albeit unintentionally. The critical lesson here is the importance of mixing it up on a daily basis. Change your style of delivery; change the assignments; change the groups; re-arrange the classroom. This is the single best way to engage Gen-Next students in the classroom setting.

Establishing Rapport with Students

As much of an impact as communication modes can have when used in a classroom setting, they can have an even bigger impact in one-on-one interactions. As a teacher, it's very valuable to be able to recognize in what mode students are operating, as this will increase your chances of connecting and building rapport with each. By building rapport with them, you greatly increase your chances of engaging them and empowering them to learn.

So, to be a master educator, you must master the **Six Major Elements of Building Rapport:**

1. **Match the modality** that the student is exhibiting. Whenever communicating with a highly visual student, sit up in your chair, breathe from the top of your lungs, and be excited. If you're with an auditory student, slow down a bit, modulate your voice more and listen – *really* listen. And if you're interacting with a student with a strong kinesthetic tendency, slow waaaay dooown, and talk to them about their feelings.

2. **Physically mirror** the individual's physiology. Aim to physically copy their posture, facial expressions, hand gestures and movements. Their eye-blinking will cause their body to say unconsciously to their mind, "Hey, she's

like me!" It's undeniable to the nervous system.

3. Match their voice: the tone, tempo, timbre (quality of the voice) and volume. You can also match their key words. Perhaps they often say, "Actually"; if so, use it several times when talking with them.

4. Match their breathing. Strive to pace the student's breathing – breathe at exactly the same time (matching inhalations and exhalations). Doing this can help you to lead them out of the "mode" they are in and into another one.

5. Match the size of the pieces of information (chunk size or level of abstraction) in which they seem most comfortable. If a student tends to covet "the big picture," he or she will probably be bored with minute details, and conversely.

6. Match their common experiences. Aim to find commonalities with each student: common interests, background, beliefs, values and ideologies. This is a huge component of building rapport.

Keys to Communication:
S.U.C.C.E.S.S.

Apply the following characteristics to ensure successful communication:

Sensitivity *to differences in culture, ideas, opinions and learning styles.*

Understanding *and exhibiting empathy and open-mindedness in dealing with all students.*

Caring *for and nurturing students' results in more than just a teacher-student relationship.*

Choice *empowers students in a way dictatorship cannot.*

Esteem *is a powerful asset for a developing mind, so look for opportunities to build confidence.*

Sharing *and working as a team allows students to celebrate successes together.*

Silence *truly is golden, especially when you listen, listen, listen.*

Conflict Management:

Theory X – The Story of Sue, James & Bertha

Sue was a Southern Belle who'd been teaching in south Georgia for over 30 years.

When she first started out as a teacher, she was on a mission to help every student, and she truly believed that she was going to be the teacher that all the students loved, thought was cool and would call mom. They would listen to everything she said, obey all the rules and have smiles planted on their faces as they entered the classroom each day.

But she had a difficult student named James, who knew exactly how to push Sue's buttons, and insisted on doing so at every opportunity. No matter how many times she asked him to stop, James would disrupt the class every time her back was turned.

Finally, at the end of the first week, she snapped and sent James to the principal's office. He came back 20 minutes later with his head down and handed her a note before taking his seat and putting his head on his desk.

She looked at the note from the principal:

GIVE HIM 5 LICKS.

She couldn't believe it. Staring at the paper, she thought to herself, "I can't do this. I can't hurt a child. No way! This isn't what I signed up for!" After a moment,

Sue excused herself from the class and ran next door to explain the situation to the teacher of that classroom, hyperventilating at the thought that she would have to do this, and demanding a better way to reprimand this child.

The other teacher reached under her desk and pulled out a custom made paddle called Bertha that had air holes drilled into it. She handed it to Sue, saying, "You have to do it or you will never gain control of your class. The students are testing you and what you do now will set the tone for the rest of the year." By this time, Sue was shaking.

Together, the two teachers called James out into the hallway, and the neighbor told him to stand with his hands against the wall. She held out Bertha, and reluctantly Sue grasped the paddle with her hand, took a backswing and released her first blow against his bottom. She reared back and took another swing. She started thinking to herself, "This kind of feels good," as she smacked him a third, fourth and fifth time.

Finally she instructed him to go back into the classroom and sit down. She felt relief and made her way back into the class, where all of her students had the look of terror in their eyes. James laid his head on his desk, sobbing.

Sue slunk down into her chair and burst into tears, which soon turned to anger as she wondered why the principal would ask her to do such a thing.

And then she noticed the piece of paper lying on her desk:

GAVE HIM 5 LICKS

"Does that say *GIVE* or *GAVE?*" she wondered. Sure enough, it said the latter, so after five licks from the principal, she had given him five more.

But from that moment on, James was far and away the best, brightest and most well-behaved student she would have in over 30 years of teaching.

We can't do that today. We must learn to develop "win-win" relationships that foster cooperation.

THE FIESE SYSTEM OF CONFLICT RESOLUTION

Conflict is inevitable. One of the most challenging – and certainly least enjoyable – jobs of a coach is calling students out when they haven't done their work or when they behave inappropriately. But this is a key part of the job – professional athletes are constantly getting benched, fired, fined, assigned extra work-outs or otherwise punished by their coaches for violating team rules. Without enforcing the rules, the coach would be completely unable to maintain order, which is critical to success.

80% of all problems stem from poor, or lack of, communication!

Remember, though, that you can't rule Gen-Next kids with an iron fist. For some kids, the threat of detention or visiting the principal may work, but for many, it's just an unfortunate consequence of maintaining their reputation. So the trick to maintaining order in the class is to *empower your students* to choose their fate.

To help teachers effectively manage conflict in the classroom, I developed the *Fiese System of Conflict Resolution* a few years ago. The system is composed of three key steps:

1) **Confront**
2) **Discipline**
3) **Recover**

STEP 1 – CONFRONT

When faced with classroom conflict, you have to take control from the get-go by being assertive – not authoritarian – and communicating with tact and skill. One of the most powerful communication tools available when confronting conflict is what I call the E.A.S.Y. Script – a four-part process (see below) used to diffuse conflict quickly and develop a win-win relationship.

When faced with conflict, it's a case of "fight or flight." We fight back using ego and emotion, or become passive and let others walk over us. Neither is good. The E.A.S.Y. Script removes ego and emotion (the true cause of conflict) from the communication process and enables you to be assertive and develop a win-win relationship.

E.A.S.Y. SCRIPT

Express how you feel. This is a retreat statement, stopping whatever actions are currently in progress to address the situation at hand. Use non-baggage words, and be clear and concise, avoiding modifiers, qualifiers or amplifiers.

Assess the situation. This is a reevaluation statement, used to alert the target to the reason for the confrontation. Deal with specifics, and avoid using phrases like "because you" that assign fault or blame.

State your expectation. This is a re-approach statement, used to tell the student what you want from them. Be specific and reasonable.

Yes/No question. This is a handshake statement, to make sure the student understands the expectation, and is used as part of the pre-discipline process. Only ask questions that can be answered with a yes or no.

THE E.A.S.Y. SCRIPT IN ACTION

You tell a disruptive student to stop talking, but the student continues anyway. You tell the student again to stop talking. A minute later, the student begins chattering away again. While your initial impulse might be to lash out and tell the student if he or she doesn't stop talking, he or she is going straight to the principal's office. Instead, however, use the E.A.S.Y. Script approach:

1) Express to the student exactly how you feel:
"I'm shocked!"

LEVELS OF CONFLICT

Look for the warning signs of conflict, and step in before it escalates to the next level.

Level 1: Disagreement – *Occurs when two or more people have differing opinions; can usually be settled through communication.*

Level 2: Resentment – *Parties begin to hold their ground; communication diminishes.*

Level 3: Hostility – *Communication drops almost entirely, and physical altercation is on the horizon.*

Whenever there is group conflict in the classroom, you as teacher need to serve as a competent and objective negotiator or mediator – listening closely to both sides of "the story" and facilitating open, constructive communication without taking sides. It's up to you to guide the opposing sides toward an agreeable solution – a win/win.

2) Assess (reevaluate the situation):

"I have told you to stop talking and you have continued to ignore my request."

3) State your expectation:

"I need you to turn around, face forward and begin working on your assignment now."

4) Yes/No question:

"Is that clear?"

STEP 2: DISCIPLINE/CONSEQUENCES

You follow the E.A.S.Y. Script by explaining to the student what the consequences will be if his/her negative behavior continues:

"If you continue to talk, here is what will happen: You will be assigned to detention. If your disruptive talking continues even after a detention, you will have to go to speak with the principal about this problem."

What you have done is removed your ego and emotion by using the E.A.S.Y. Script, and importantly, you have given the student the power of choice – they have the opportunity to determine their own outcome. Most students, if given the choice, will choose the outcome that benefits them the most. If they do not, your job is simple – enforce the disciplinary action that you clearly presented, while staying in control and not coming off as an emotional hothead.

The E.A.S.Y. Script is a particularly useful approach with Gen-Nexters, who generally speaking, do not respond well to intimidation and authoritarian rule in the classroom. With this script in hand, you uphold your authority while still giving students an option, thus helping to empower them.

Of course, things don't always go according to "script"; you will sometimes be faced with deflectors – people who do not want to take responsibility for their actions. For example: Let's say you have a student who is often late to class. You decide to *confront* the student (Step 1 of the Fiese System of Conflict Resolution) using the E.A.S.Y. Script:

I'm concerned. On a number of occasions you have come in late to my class. I expect you to be in your seat when the bell rings, no questions asked. Do you understand?

The student replies:

Ego + Emotion = Aggression

I'm never late to class.

You can now use what's called a *rollover* statement by repeating parts 3 and 4:

I expect you to be in your seat when the bell rings, no questions asked. Do you understand?

The student replies:

Yeah, but....

Roll it over again, but this time include the progressive discipline step:

I expect you to be in your seat when the bell rings, no questions asked. If not, you will get a detention; and if the problem continues, you will be sent to the principal's office.

STEP 3 – RECOVERY

The final step in the Fiese System of Conflict Resolution involves repairing the relationship between you and the student(s), with an emphasis on student empowerment. This is absolutely critical, in order to prevent the build-up of resentment, which kills motivation.

I have devised a three-part *Recovery Script* (that, by the way, can be used with both students and parents) to assist in this effort:

1) Acknowledge the student's perspective. Be empathetic

Ten Tactics for Keeping the Lines of Communication Open

1. *Ask questions.*
2. *Continually work on listening skills.*
3. *Show enthusiasm & excitement.*
4. *Use compliments freely & easily.*
5. *Smile often.*
6. *Avoid absolutes (like "always" or "never").*
7. *Be attuned to other people's communication styles.*
8. *Be mindful of your body language.*
9. *Be available.*
10. *Communicate often.*

toward the student's viewpoint or reasoning, but maintain control. Using the example of the student who often arrives late to class, you might approach the student after class, delve a little deeper, and say something like, "Ok, I understand you have to take your brother to school and then find a parking space, but arriving to my class late each day is unacceptable."

2) Ask an open-ended question. The purpose here is to empower the student to come up with a suitable solution. For example: "What can you do to make sure you're not late to my class?" Wait for the student to elicit such viable answers as, "Leave my house 10 minutes earlier," or "Not stopping by my locker before coming to class."

3) Acceptance and agreement. Confirm that the student agrees to abide by the acceptable solution(s) he or she has offered: "Ok, that sounds like a good solution. Is this something we can agree on?"

Using this system greatly increases your chances of altering negative behavior and conflict in the classroom. By making students part of the solution, and by taking time to assess situations before rigidly handing out punishment, you empower students to improve rather than blindly boss them around and embarrass them before their peers. Students typically want to do well and behave well for teachers they respect and admire.

And the way to earn their respect and admiration is to master the multi-layered art of communication.

KEY POINTS TO REMEMBER

• *Eighty percent of a teacher's time in the classroom should be spent listening.*

• *Only 7% of your communication comes from your words. Thirty-eight percent comes from your tone of voice and 55% comes from your body language.*

• *A person can only listen for 15 seconds before they consciously or subconsciously stop.*

• *Active listening refers to physical body language, while reflective listening is listening to the content of the message.*

• *To listen effectively in the classroom, ask a pointed question, followed by an open-ended question, followed by a reflective question.*

• *There are three modes of communication: visual (person tends* to looks up); auditory (person looks to the sides) and kinesthetic (person looks down).

• *There are six brain functions: authoritative (task-oriented and structured); deductive (analytical/logical); emotional (social); intuitive (act on intuition); sensory (use all senses) and test-driver (goal- and journey-oriented).*

• *There are two dimensions of personal communication style: direct/indirect (more/less assertive) and supporting/controlling (more/less expressed).*

• *Change your lesson plan, assignments, etc. on a daily basis to incorporate all modes, brain functions and personal communication styles in the classroom.*

• *In one-on-one communication, match the modality, physicality, voice, breathing, information size and common experiences for the person you're communicating with.*

• *When you find yourself needing to resolve conflict with a student, first **confront** the student using the E.A.S.Y. Script (express how you feel, assess the situation, state your expectation, yes/no question), then apply progressive **discipline/consequences** to give the student a choice regarding their action, and then apply the **recovery** script (acknowledge the student's perspective, ask an open-ended question, acceptance/agreement) and empower them in the future.*

Chapter 5
Motivating @ a Million bps

Don't Go with the Flow – Get into It

Most people, when directly asked, will say that they would prefer to have more free time than to go to work. But have you ever noticed what happens when they actually get that free time? When people retire, they do one of three things: take on a "retirement job", pursue the extracurricular activities they didn't have time for when they were working or die of boredom. The phenomenon is similar in working adults who have been out of the office for too long, and it's the same thing with students at the end of summer vacation. You can only vacation for a few weeks at a time before you're ready to go back to work.

Croatian psychologist Mihály Csíkszentmihályi, in his seminal work, *Flow: The Psychology of Optimal Experience*, tells us why: **People are most happy, energetic and productive when they are in a state of flow.**

It makes perfect sense. People who are in a state of flow are fully immersed in what they are doing; they experience a strong feeling of energized focus, of full involvement, and are wholly committed to the success of the activity or project in which they are engaged. Not only is there a sense of satisfaction that comes with completing the task, there's a simple time equation involved: If all your mental energy is focused on this one thing, your mental energy isn't being spent worrying about something else.

According to Csíkszentmihályi, the flow state is an optimal state of *intrinsic motivation*. In an interview with Wired magazine, Csíkszentmihályi described flow as "being completely involved in an activity for its own sake.

Keys to Motivation: Components of Flow

Csíkszentmihályi identifies the following as contributing to and/or accompanying an experience of flow:

- *Clear goals*
- *Concentrating and focusing*
- *Loss of self-consciousness*
- *Time seems to slow down or speed up*
- *Direct and immediate feedback*
- *Balance between challenge and ability*
- *Control*
- *Intrinsic reward*
- *Absorption in the activity*

The ego falls away. Time flies. Every action, movement and thought follows inevitably from the previous one, like playing jazz. Your whole being is involved, and you're using your skills to the utmost."

We often hear sports announcers use phrases like "in the zone" or "on fire" to describe an athlete who is performing at a remarkably high level in a game or match. But how often do your students experience this level of flow in the classroom?

Well, as their coach, it's now your job to get them into that zone.

Education + Entertainment = Motivation

EXTRINSIC AND INTRINSIC MOTIVATION

EXTRINSIC MOTIVATION

Extrinsic motivation is the pursuit of some tactile external reward that has been promised for completing or accomplishing a particular task or assignment. It also refers to actions driven by the threat of punishment for failing to complete that task. Positive reinforcement works far better than negative reinforcement, so look for creative ways to acknowledge students for a job well done, rather than waiting to punish them when they do something wrong.

Public praise – whether in the form of a pizza party, a

CREATIVE IDEAS FOR EXTRINSIC MOTIVATION

Below are some ideas to get you thinking about creative ways to reward your students for a job well done. Don't stick to these; come up with your own ideas that work for your students and your class.

• Cite accomplishments in the school newsletter or on the school's web site.

• Organize a pizza party as a thank you for a particularly strong effort.

• Have a group of deserving students represent the class at a faculty meeting or other event.

• Present plaques or framed certificates of achievement to students who have gone "above and beyond."

• Hold a Student Appreciation Day and hand out awards.

• Give free time at the end of class for completing work well and efficiently.

• Create a "Wall of Fame".

• Give handwritten "Thank you" notes to students who have helped fellow students and/or helped you be a better teacher.

"Wall of Fame," or a book that compiles their best essays of the year – is a great motivator. By praising students in a way that doesn't embarrass them, but makes them feel appreciated or successful, you're both rewarding them for a job well done and providing a positive sense of self-worth.

In elementary schools, extrinsic motivation is often created with stars or toys. At the next level, it's report cards and detention. Notice that six-year-olds are usually far more excited to go to school than 15-year-olds. Now you know why. As the rewards get less tangible, less public and less positive the students start caring less.

While there's nothing wrong with extrinsic motivation, a student can be extrinsically motivated without being truly engaged or empowered – their behavior is dictated by the receipt of a reward or avoidance of punishment, and is unrelated to an internal desire to succeed at the task at hand.

That brings us to:

Intrinsic Motivation

Intrinsic motivation refers to the motivation that arises from performing an activity that is inherently – or intrinsically – satisfying. It occurs when people experience pleasure, develop a skill or morally feel it is the right thing to do. This type of motivation involves no obvious external incentives to drive behavior: it is internal, long-lasting and far more powerful and effective.

Notice that the reason public praise is such a powerful motivator is because it provides students with a positive sense of self worth – this is intrinsic motivation. If a student feels that he or she is accomplishing great things, he will naturally be inclined to work harder to accomplish those things, because it's all part of the "flow" experience.

The most successful and forward-thinking educators are much more concerned with intrinsic motivation. Intrinsically motivated students are bound to do much better in classroom activities because they are willing and eager to learn new material. Their learning experience is more meaningful, and they go deeper into the subject to fully understand it. In comparison, students who are only extrinsically motivated may have to be "bribed" to perform the same tasks.

So what, specifically, leads to high levels of intrinsic motivation in the classroom? *When what is being learned is important to the student.*

Motivation is caught, not taught.

Who Do You Work For?

In spite of the sentence with which we opened this chapter, you'll notice that you seldom hear professional athletes say they'd rather have "free time" than play a game or even go to practice. That's because they're clear who they're working for. People who complain about their jobs are unhappy because they feel their energy is spent satisfying someone else, rather than themselves.

Similarly, if students aren't inspired to go to class, it's because they feel their energy is spent satisfying the needs of everyone but themselves: their parents, their teachers, the administration, the district, the State. Where does the student come in? What's in it for them?

Well, to teach Gen-Next students, you need to be able to answer that question – "What's in it for me?" – for every task your students are being assigned. Approach every lesson with an attitude of assisting the learner in obtaining accomplishments that are valuable to *them*. Teach every student from the context of how this lesson will help them integrate themselves into the world, or relate better with others, or promote their own self-awareness or achieve their dreams.

Your job as teacher is to create a contagious classroom environment in which students naturally hunger for

Intrinsic motivation is a far stronger motivator than extrinsic motivation; however, external motivation can easily displace intrinsic motivation. Make sure you're always clear on which one you're using.

knowledge and feel inspired to continually improve. It's to create opportunities that are highly conducive to learning, inspiration and exploration. This is what we mean when we say that motivation is *caught*, not taught.

A funny thing happens when you do this: students start disciplining each other. If students are excited to be in class and to learn whatever is in front of them, they stop laughing when people misbehave, because it just distracts them from this activity that they're enjoying. Acting up in class disappears, because the negative reinforcement – disapproval of inappropriate behavior – comes from the student's peers, rather than from an authority figure.

One last thing on this topic. Just because your focus should be on intrinsic motivation doesn't mean extrinsic motivation isn't valuable. The key is not to fall into the all-too-common trap of letting extrinsic rewards displace the intrinsic ones. In other words, be careful not to set the expectation among students that they will get something special every time they do something well, because then they stop doing the work for themselves and start doing it only for the reward.

PROVIDING INTRINSIC MOTIVATION

THE BURGER TECHNIQUE

One highly effective tool that teachers have at their disposal to help enhance intrinsic motivation is called the Burger Technique. I recommend that you use this technique at least 15 times a day:

Think of a hamburger:

Step 1: Whenever a student behaves in a positive manner or does something that you would like to see more of in the future, tell the student specifically what they did, and be specific about why you are praising them.

Step 2: Tell the student how their behavior/actions made you feel; this makes it personal and real. It's always a good thing to share your emotion with others when those emotions are positive and true.

105

PRINCIPLES OF MOTIVATION

Who you are is more important than the techniques you use.

People respond to a clear, compelling vision.

Effective communication is essential to trust – and to motivation.

Fear inhibits action and hampers motivation.

Listening fosters buy-in and support.

People tend to live up to expectations.

Sincere recognition goes a long way.

People are motivated by interesting and fun work.

People want to be involved and have a reasonable degree of autonomy.

Most people have yet-to-be discovered talents that can help drive them.

Personal growth and development is inspiring.

Personal problems debilitate enthusiasm and performance.

Good working (classroom/school) conditions create good vibes.

Tactful discipline earns respect and fosters commitment.

Step 3: Tell the student the outcomes of their actions – how their positive behavior benefits them. (This is usually an extrinsic motivation statement.)

Here's an example to help clarify the Burger Technique: Let's say I have a student who is on the golf team and who travels a lot – often missing class, but still managing to turn everything in on time and maintaining an "A" in the class. Merely telling the student "Good job!" is fine, but not very motivating or empowering. What if, on the other hand, you use the Burger Technique:

"The fact that you have missed six days of class and have still managed to get your work in on time and hold an 'A' in my class is fantastic! It makes me feel wonderful

106

to teach a student who works so hard and wants to learn. Your work ethic and dedication is going to help you become extremely successful in whatever profession you get into."

Now, that type of feedback sticks. You made a valuable and motivational deposit in the student's "mental bank account" – a deposit that is very likely to inspire further positive behavior and action by the student. The child with a lot of deposits in his mental bank account doesn't cause problems in class, because he wants to please the person who's making him feel good.

The real power of the Burger Technique is that it focuses on the positive rather than the negative. The average American receives 432 negative messages a day and only 32 positive ones, so by providing students with personalized and authentic praise, recognition and acknowledgment, you're bridging the gap, building self-esteem and making all the difference in the child's attitude.

Stewardship Delegation: Creating Self-Generated Motivation

It's important not only to recognize and acknowledge the positive actions and behaviors that students exhibit, but also to empower them to take on new challenges and provide them with a strong sense of accomplishment. As a teacher, coach and mentor, you have the power to instill in students a high level of confidence and the desire to tackle a variety of meaningful projects and tasks.

Unfortunately, many teachers fail to recognize this power, and instead of guiding students toward meaningful accomplishments, they coldly delegate mundane tasks that students must complete. How many times have you seen or heard of a teacher start the class period simply by telling students what they "have to do"? The teacher provides the students with some general outline and then tells them to get to work. This is called "gopher" delegation: "Go do this," "Go do that," or "Here's what I need you to do." This type of delegation does not work. You might think you're delegating and saving time, but the students have no buy-in or ownership, and thus no motivation. Consequently, you'll end up having to ride students and continuously check their work (and maybe even complete it for them) because – due to gopher delegation – they are not driven or inspired to complete the tasks at hand on their own accord.

There is only one type of effective delegation, and that is *stewardship delegation*. Created by Stephen Covey in *The 7 Habits of Highly Effective People*, stewardship delegation is a management technique that has been adopted by businesses all over the world, and with good reason. It fosters intrinsic motivation and is the essence of facilitated learning and what it is to be a Theory C teacher. Here is how it works.

Step 1: Share the vision – explain the task(s) and desired goal(s) in detail.

Step 2: Ask the students how they will complete the task. Empower, don't enforce. Get rid of the "gopher."

Step 3: Share the importance of the work/task. Discuss the big picture – the value and scope of the impact that students stand to make.

Step 4: Set accountability checkpoints. This helps to

guide – but not drag – the students in the right direction and ensure that each person understands his or her role.

Here's an example of stewardship delegation in action:

Step 1: "Class, today our goal is to learn about supply and demand. You will be divided up into groups and will read the case study of a local company. Your objective is to come up with a way to increase demand for their products and then stand up and deliver a two-minute speech.

Step 2: "How are you going to go about this?" (Listen to each group's ideas, and provide guidance.)

Step 3: "This lesson is so important because it provides you with the understanding of how to grow a company and make more money. This will help you when you get into the real world. You may own your own business or work for a company that faces the same challenge. The more experience you have, the better equipped you'll be to make the right decisions."

Step 4: "Alright, you know what you're supposed to do and what needs to be done by the end of class. So, at 12:30, you should already have your strategy and begin working on the delivery. I will be walking around to help those who need it."

The best teachers use stewardship delegation in lessons and projects every day to motivate students and create a strong sense of self-worth and responsibility. The technique works because you introduce a goal, get

To teach is to touch lives forever.

students actively involved in the planning and decision-making, get them into that critical state of flow and ensure that they understand the importance of what they are working on, giving them a feasible deadline that sets them up for success. This is facilitated learning.

You Have the Chance to Be <u>That</u> Teacher

You hold the key to sustained motivation and performance in the classroom. But you need more than an idealistic perspective and lots of energy and enthusiasm to truly move tomorrow's movers and shakers; you need insight and strategy. Embracing the key principles covered in this chapter and incorporating the varied proven techniques for inspiring and empowering your students will enable you to get students excited about learning and exploring, and about their future and the infinite possibilities that lie before them.

When star students go on to achieve great things, what teacher doesn't want to be the one remembered whenever they look back on the people who influenced, challenged and supported them the most in their lives? If you consistently follow the practices and tactics touted in this chapter, you will almost certainly be that teacher to countless students who were fortunate enough to pass through your classroom.

Key Points to Remember

• *People are most happy, energetic and productive when they are in a state of flow, and it's your job as a teacher to put them there.*

• *Extrinsic motivation is a response to a tactile external reward or punishment for completing or failing to complete an assignment. Intrinsic motivation refers to engagement in an activity because it provides pleasure, develops a skill or is morally the right thing to do.*

• *Intrinsic motivation occurs in today's classroom when the teacher creates a classroom environment that is highly conducive to learning, inspiration and exploration. This should be the primary focus of a Gen-Next teacher.*

• *The Burger Technique is a tool for praising students in a way that provides intrinsic motivation. Tell the student what they did, how their actions made you feel and what the outcomes of their actions are.*

• *Stewardship delegation is a way to assign tasks to students while motivating them intrinsically. Share the vision, empower the students to generate ideas for accomplishing the assignment, offer a big-picture discussion of how it will benefit them and set accountability checkpoints.*

Neutralizing Negativity

Negativity – in the form of anger, fear, worry, hurt, laziness or envy – is always a sign of discouragement. Common causes are avoiding domination, low self-esteem, seeking attention, stress, boredom and resentment for an action perceived as unfair.

There are three types of "nega-holics":

• **Behavioral:** *Possess a fear of success (with success comes change, and with change comes fear, uncertainty and doubt), so set themselves up for failure.*
• **Mental:** *Perfectionists who cannot live up to their own demands, and thus no one else can. They set unrealistic expectations, causing others to become discouraged.*
• **Verbal:** *Everything out of their mouth is pessimistic.*

Changing the behavior of nega-holics is difficult, but not impossible. Make each one aware of their "condition" and tell them how it negatively affects not only their own performance, but also that of their peers. Then, offer exercises and tactics to help them oust the negative demons within them, including (but not limited to) the following:

Recognize that all hurtful experiences are stepping-stones; not stumbling blocks. *With conflict comes growth. Encourage students to learn from bad experiences, to take lessons away from struggle and to use the anger and energy generated by conflict to fuel them. Cite examples of successful people who have accomplished greatness following notable failure. (Abraham Lincoln is a great example.)*
Look for the positive in all negative situations. *This may smack of pure Pollyanna fluff, but there is something positive to take away and learn from all negative events. Inspire students to become detectives of optimism by modeling one in class.*
Scream the negative thoughts out of your head. *Sometimes the loudest, most productive shouts don't make a sound. Learn to – and instruct students to – fend off pessimistic notions by hollering internally. You'd be surprised how effective a good brain scream can be.*
Interrupt your current thought pattern. *Remember from Chapter 1 – people behave based on their thoughts, and can change behavior and their immediate universe by changing their mindset. While easier said than done, teach students how to recognize when negativity is taking over their mind and show them how to respond by "de-catastrophizing."*

A Story of Empowerment

Bob had been teaching for 25 years at an alternative school for people with special needs. His students were diagnosed with Asperger's , autism, Attention-Deficit/Hyperactivity Disorder and other severe learning disabilities, and all needed special attention in order to learn.

When he started, he was really good at it. His students liked him, they connected with him and he had a great track record in sending them on to assimilate successfully into society. But over time, things had begun to disintegrate.

Some of the students shouted or talked through class. One would stand up and pace, because that was his method of coping. And where Bob used to be able to use his authority to threaten discipline for acting out, that method didn't work anymore.

He started yelling at his students. His frustration began to

113

grow. In short, he was turning into the teacher he never wanted to be, and was seriously considering "retirement," because he couldn't handle the stress anymore.

Then, on a whim, one of the directors at the school decided to send him to one of my seminars. And with great relief, he realized that his frustration had nothing to do with him.

It wasn't that he was turning into a jerk or was a less effective teacher than he used to be. The reason he was getting frustrated was because the techniques he'd used 25 years ago, on late Baby Boomers and early Gen-X students, weren't the things that worked on Gen-Next kids. It wasn't he who changed, it was the generation.

So when he went home, he started to work on some of the principles and techniques he'd learned. He resolved to mentor students instead of acting as a dictator. Instead of yelling at them, he used the E.A.S.Y. Script. Instead of focusing on discipline, he focused on communication and creating a bond.

The difference was night and day. His students responded immediately to the change, and Bob was once again motivated and excited about life. Before long, other teachers recognized the change and started asking him what happened. And within a few years, the school had adopted these techniques as an institution-wide practice.

SECTION III
BUILDING YOUR GAME PLAN:
Teaching in the Modern Era

Consider the difference between a class that's being lectured at and one in which the students are actively involved, debating each other and coming up with their own solutions, while you are acting simply as the moderator. I know which class I'd rather be in.

Chapter 6
Edutainment

The days of standing statically at the front of the class delivering lectures and asking students to sit quietly and take notes are long gone. This is the Age of Empowerment.

Edutainment is interactive, experiential learning that entertains during the education process.

Two of the key characteristics of Generation Next are fluency with technology and an expectation of amusement. It started with Baby Einstein and toys that talk when you touch them, and then moved into Blues Clues and Sesame Street. Then, as soon as they could read and write, they were accessing the Internet for all the YouTube and MySpace they could get.

In short, from the time these kids were born, their education came from technology, and it came with an expectation of amusement, and they expect that to continue. If you try to educate them without any of the above, you're fighting an uphill battle against students who are bored to tears.

FACILITATED LEARNING

As promising as Generation Next is, one area in which they have ample room for improvement is interpersonal communication. Because Gen-Nexters have pretty much been wired since birth, most are more adept at short message system (SMS), text chat and e-mail than they are at holding a conversation with another human being.

This is a concern, not only because it affects how well they can communicate with teachers, parents/relatives, bosses and other members of more verbally communicative generations; but also because, according to recent research, poor interpersonal communication skills can cause feelings of alienation, isolation, anxiety and depression.

According to Csíkszentmihályi, the happiest time in a person's life is when they are communicating one-on-one with someone they love, enjoy being around and respect. Thus, text-obsessed members of Generation Next are missing out on a vital component of happiness and the human experience.

So as an educator, you need to get back to the basics – to empower students via effective, dynamic communication. Today's students, more than any preceding generation, need to learn to embrace verbal communication in the classroom and to feel the "touch" of their teacher.

But remember, you're dealing with Gen-Nexters – an entire generation raised on complex and visually stunning video games, powerful Web-enabled computers and televisions featuring hundreds of channels. Thus, if you want to truly enthrall, inspire and empower today's students, you must deliver intriguing content in a highly engaging manner.

Note that eliminating technology entirely is not necessary, in fact, you may find that students' confidence in you will increase if you use technological means of education from time to time, because it's bringing them something they know and understand to teach them something new. But it's important that you don't rely on technology and special effects to create an alluring classroom for students.

Neither, for that matter, is it necessary to juggle polygons with your feet in order to teach your students geometry. All this means is that you need to learn how to engage and empower your students in class. Make *them* do the work, while you do what you're paid to do: Listen.

LISTENING:

THE KEY TO FACILITATED LEARNING

I recently met a young man who described to me the most memorable teacher he ever had. She taught U.S. history, but her class was unlike that of any other history teacher he'd experienced.

From day one, the classes were discussion-oriented. She spent very little time talking. Rather, she'd start class with an open-ended question. "Should the colonies try to sever their ties to the British Empire?" A student would raise his hand and offer his opinion. And when she saw a second student's hand shoot up at a particular comment made by the first, she'd call on him or her, who more often than not would offer a counter-point. If no counterpoint was made, she would play devil's advocate and would masterfully steer the conversation into a debate.

In some classes, the discussion would be more formalized – students would be divided into groups, and they'd develop and present their arguments in a formal debate format. In other classes, the discussion would be more characterized – one person would play Alexander Hamilton and the other Patrick Henry in a debate for and against Federalism; or everyone in the class would be assigned to play one of the attendees at the Constitutional Convention, and the class, as a unit, would generate their own U.S. Constitution.

She assigned her students far more reading than any of them were used to, and every night, her students had to answer the "short essay" questions at the end of every chapter, or do some other kind of project or assignment. But she never had a problem with students doing the work, and she never saw students yawning, looking at the clock or dozing off at their desks.

This is because her students felt truly empowered. They stayed entertained. They *wanted* to do their home-work, not because of the threat of a bad grade or of getting

10 Myths About Public Speaking

1. I am not a public speaker. Successful presenters are not born; they are made.

2. Don't talk with your hands. The natural movement of hands while speaking often conveys enthusiasm and can help to support and even drive home the meaning of key points.

3. Look over the heads of the audience. Some people believe that doing this helps to settle the speaker's nerves, but actually it just leaves the audience feeling alienated. Make eye contact.

4. Memorize your speech. Over-memorization kills passion; it clips the wings of powerful and moving improvisation.

5. Stand in one place. Remember, 55% of communication comes from body language. Move around to show your passion.

6. Always use a lectern. It's okay to have a lectern in the center of a stage or classroom – to begin your presentation and to place your notes – but don't remain married to it; otherwise, you will soon become divorced from your captive audience.

7. Cover all the points in your speech. Don't get married to your speech, because it kills active questions and engagement.

8. Start with a joke. Humor has its place, but a failed joke makes it difficult to regain your audience.

9. Shut the lights off to show slides/videos/etc. Turning the lights off takes the focus off your body language and facial expressions, and it also gives them an opportunity to doze.

10. Don't be nervous. It's completely natural to feel nervous prior to engaging in public speaking; in fact, that jittery feeling – when kept somewhat in check and managed – is what fuels the most powerful and memorable speeches.

yelled at, but because they knew if they didn't they wouldn't be able to participate in class, and they wanted to participate.

This is facilitated learning.

Notice the application of everything discussed so far in this book. Rather than talking at her students, she spends most of her time listening, so that she can guide the discussion. Notice that she uses all the representational systems – visual (reading), auditory (discussion) and kinesthetic (assignment) – to capture all the learning styles, and that classes are structured just a little differently from one to the next, in order to capture the different brain functions.

Notice how empowering it is for a student to be able to walk out of class knowing that he influenced the discussion; that he made a point no-one else made; that he was heard, understood and appreciated by his teacher and by his peers. Notice that students are entertained because they are participating in the process (remember, the Internet and video game generation expect to have control over their environment), and interacting with each other, developing not just their knowledge of history, but their communication skills as well.

Notice how all of this is intrinsically motivating – the students do their work because they get satisfaction out of it, not because they get a grade.

This is what it is to be a Theory C teacher in the 21st century.

Ten Elements of Facilitated Learning

1. Listen – As a general rule, avoid lecturing like the plague. While the occasional front-of-the-room presentation-of-materials-while-writing-on-a-chalkboard may be necessary, always look for creative ways to get your students to be the ones doing the talking. Notice I said creative ways – this does not mean asking objective questions that have a definite right or wrong answer. Students are less likely to respond or become engaged when there's a chance that they could be laughed at or look stupid for saying the wrong thing. Remember Ben Stein in *Ferris Bueller's Day Off*?

> *In 1930, the Republican-controlled House of Representatives, in an effort to alleviate the effects of the … Anyone? Anyone? … The Great Depression, passed the … Anyone? Anyone? The tariff bill? The Hawley-Smoot Tariff Act? Which … Anyone? … Raised or lowered? … Raised tariffs, in an effort to collect more revenue for the federal government. Did it work? Anyone? Anyone know the effects? … It did not work, and the United States sank deeper into the Great Depression.*
>
> *– Ferris Bueller's Day Off*

I would've skipped school, too.

2. Incorporate Different Learning and Communication Styles – Look back at Chapter 4 and think about all the different ways to describe learning and communication:

- Visual, auditory or kinesthetic
- Authoritative, deductive, emotional, intuitive, sensory or test-driver
- Direct or indirect
- Supporting or controlling

Each student uses some different combination of these modes or styles, and your job as a teacher is to incorporate all of them in whatever way you can. Math teachers, for example, almost exclusively teach kinesthetically and deductively: Students are given assignments that they must work through, and explanations are always fact-based and analytical. But some students don't work like that, and if certain students are having trouble getting it, chances are it's because they're not being related to in a way that makes sense to them.

Intuitive students need to know that the answer feels right – so give them questions that have answers that make sense, and slowly introduce them to the problems with answers that aren't quite so intuitive. Or, for the visual learners, look for ways to show, graphically, the algebraic problem and its solution, and how that solution makes sense.

3. Apply Stewardship Delegation – Break students into groups and have them work on assignments that will be of value to them. Make sure

> ## Six Voice Techniques to Keep Your Listeners Engaged
>
> **1. Increase volume** – *shows excitement and interest.*
> **2. Reduce volume/pitch** – *pulls the listener toward you.*
> **3. Vary speed** - *changes the pace to keep listeners interested.*
> **4. Stretch important words** – *to show emphasis.*
> **5. Staccato effect** – *uses pronounced pauses to emphasize important words.*
> **6. Elevator word groupings** – *when listing items or key points, increase volume or emphasis with each successive point.*

they're aware of the value, and make sure to empower them to come up with the solution. Stewardship delegation is described in more detail in Chapter 5.

4. Give Students Control – The best way to empower students in today's classroom is to give them control over the class. Asking subjective questions for discussion is a great way to do that. Asking them how they're going to accomplish their task is another biggie.

Q & A

Gen-Nexters are a naturally inquisitive lot. Encourage asking questions, as it promotes participation and provides you with an opportunity to demonstrate your knowledge and proficiency of the subject matter.

By the same token, though, avoid the most common mistakes when answering questions:

- *Answering too much*
- *Answering too soon*
- *Having a long dialogue with just one person*

But it doesn't have to stop there. Letting them choose their lesson plan – what to learn about, how to learn it and even what their assignment should be – promotes leadership and initiative and gives the students a sense of ownership over their education. Obviously, this particular suggestion can only be applied to a certain extent, but it's the premise that's important.: A student who has control over his education is far more intrinsically motivated than one who's forced into doing an assignment he doesn't care about.

To take it a step further, offer students control over you as a teacher. Some schools implement student teacher evaluations as a matter of course, but many wait until the end of the year, when it can no longer impact the class you're teaching right now. Asking your students for feedback is invaluable to your learning and developing as a teacher, and it also gives your students a sense of ownership over your class. Ask them (usually anonymously) what they would like to see from you or from the class, and make every effort to put that into practice as soon as possible.

5. Change It Up – Gen-Nexters have short attention spans. Think about the lightning pace of TV-shows, movies, of music videos, the Internet and YouTube. Pen pals are now AIM buddies – if you want to talk to someone halfway around the world, you no longer need to wait two weeks for the next installment of the conversation.

Things change quickly in this technologically-driven world, and your classroom should be no different. If you want to keep your students' attention, strive to have every class different than the one before it. Certainly the content will be different, but add to that, the structure or learning styles. Changing up the pace of the classroom will keep your students engaged and interested as they continue to learn.

LAUGHING MATTERS

When used appropriately, humor can be a powerful tool for capturing the attention of and eliciting enthusiasm from students during a classroom presentation. But if used inappropriately, it can ruin an entire class. Some tips:

*• **Don't try too hard**. It's more important for a teacher to see funny than it is to be funny. In other words, laughing with your students is far more important than trying to make your students laugh.*

*• **Avoid making trite jokes**. The best humor is observational and spontaneous and calls out the absurdity of day-to-day life.*

*• **Avoid** (and don't tolerate) tasteless or offensive humor – particularly sexist, racist, sexual-orientation, or religious humor.*

6. Play to Students' Strengths – Every student is good at something. But just as you may not have recognized their communication style, you may have yet to realize where their strengths are. Some are better at essays, others are better at tests. Some prefer writing assignments; others prefer artsy projects, others multiple-choice or objective answer questions. Some learn best when they're reading; others learn best through discussion. Your job is to look for each student's strength and play to that. Early on, focus your energy on praising the student for a job well done in that particular area that is his or her strength. This builds confidence and motivation. Then, gradually introduce the other areas as places where they would benefit from development. Always be sure to come back to – and acknowledge – their strengths, in order to encourage them, but remember, your job is not to coddle them, but to push/pull them to work harder.

7. Encourage Questions – I don't know any teachers in this day and age, who actively discourage their students from asking questions, but you may be doing so without even realizing it. Many students won't ask questions in front of the class – or even come to you after class – for fear of looking stupid. So, come up with creative ways to encourage questions. A sex-ed teacher that I once talked to handled this delicate and embarrassing topic by having every student write at least two questions on a piece of paper, which they placed in a box on their way out. The questions were then sorted by topic and answered the next day. This is a great tactic, not only because it eliminates the embarrassment factor, but because it forces everyone to ask questions, which gets them involved and stimulates their thought processes.

8. Use Class Time Effectively – Don't have students do in class, something they can just as easily do at home.

127

What's the point? Instead, use class time for things that can only be done in class: discussions, labs, presentations and so on.

9. Acknowledge Effort – We touched on this with the Burger Technique and will go into more detail in the next chapter, but it's a key component of the facilitated class to acknowledge effort where effort has been put forth. A simple "good work" or "excellent point" goes a long way toward motivating a student to stay involved.

10. Make It Fun – It's called edutainment for a reason. It's supposed to be fun. Projects should be entertaining as well as educational. Assignments should be interesting. If you find a student looking bored in class, it's because he's not having fun, so start looking for ways to engage him. Encourage joking around in the classroom – as long as it doesn't get out of hand. Jokes actually lighten the mood and keep people interested in participating.

Using Technology in the Classroom

Think about all the ways that the average 16-year-old might use technology on a daily basis that didn't exist thirty years ago:

- A digital alarm clock – or perhaps a cell phone or computer – wakes him up in the morning.
- On the bus ride to school, he listens to a new song by an unknown band on his iPod.
- He surreptitiously text messages his friends in class – especially when he's bored.
- During lunch, he calls his friends to find out where they are seated in the cafeteria.
- When he gets home, he and his friends furiously IM each other for about half an hour.

- While typing his essay in Microsoft Word, he looks to Thesaurus.com to find another word for "secret," ultimately settling on "surreptitious." If he needs any information for that essay, he looks it up on Wikipedia.
- For dinner, his mom says she wants to try a new restaurant. He uses his phone to look for suggestions on where to eat.
- After dinner, he turns on Tivo to watch last night's episode of *The Daily Show*.
- And then, he uses the "sleep" function on his alarm clock to let the radio lull him to sleep.

This is just the beginning, and like it or not, this is the world your students live in. Although you should do your best to expand their capacity for interpersonal communication, using educational technology to supplement the facilitated learning environment can be extremely valuable to the extensive "change-up" that's required to keep your students interested. It also helps create respect and rapport (students don't like knowing more than the person who teaches them), and it can make your job a lot easier.

E-learning is a fast-growing and incredibly complex industry. According to studies from the Sloan Consortium, on-line participation in higher education more than doubled between 2002 and 2006 – from 1.6 million to 3.5 million participants.

But e-learning describes a vast range of possibilities:

• **Instructional design** – The traditional, though electronic, method of teaching in which there is a focused curriculum developed by a single teacher or centralized learning institution.

• **Research** – It started with Encarta and ballooned from there. Now, everyone uses the Internet for research.

• **Social-constructivist applications** – Describes the use of collectivist methods like blogs, discussion forums, "wikis," etc., in which participants may askquestions, offer comments and otherwise act as full participants in the seek-and-find of knowledge acquisition.

A number of different perspectives inform the development of e-learning applications:

• **Cognitive** – Incorporates NLP or other brain-function technology in an effort to maximize learningpotential.

• **Emotional** – Accesses emotions to ensure motivation, engagement, fun, etc. in the e-learning process.

• **Behavioral** – Focuses on skills and behavioral outcomes, using tactics like role-playing or site-specific incidents.

• **Contextual** – Addresses the environmental and social elements that stimulate learning, including human interaction, collaborative discovery and peer support and pressure.

And even beyond that, there are countless ways to incorporate technology just from a logistical standpoint:

• Gone are the days of writing students' grades in a lesson planner. Now, it goes into an Excel spreadsheet or a content management system.

• Have your students e-mail you their homework, if they're willing or able.

• Actively use the Internet to look up information – or have your students look up the answers to any questions they might have.

• Make yourself available to your students for an hour every evening via AIM, so they can ask any questions they have with the homework.

• Incorporate blogging into their writing assignments.

These are just a few examples. The important thing here is not the technique itself, but to tie the unfamiliar to the familiar, to build confidence from your students and to take advantage of the opportunities technology affords us.

Note that this is a bonus, not a requirement, and that a failed attempt by an unsavvy teacher to incorporate technology in the classroom could easily backfire. What's more important is tolerance and acceptance of the technology that they use in their everyday lives. That said, it's a good way to step out of your comfort zone, which can be great for motivation, as we saw in Chapter 3.

Key Points to Remember

• *Edutainment is interactive, experiential learning that entertains during the education process.*

• *Facilitated learning applies the basics of communication in a way that is engaging to students, offering them the opportunity to interact with each other.*

• *The most important component of facilitated learning is to spend 80% of your time listening.*

• *The ten elements of facilitated learning are:*
  1. *Listen.*
  2. *Incorporate different learning and communication styles.*
  3. *Apply stewardship delegation.*
  4. *Give students control.*
  5. *Change it up.*
  6. *Play to your students' strengths.*
  7. *Encourage questions.*
  8. *Use class time effectively.*
  9. *Acknowledge effort.*
  10. *Make it fun.*

• *Although it's important to give students the opportunity to interact on an interpersonal level, you can use technology selectively to tie lessons back to what the students already know.*

Chapter 7
Praise Me, Now!
The Need for Instant Gratification

Positive Reinforcement

A hundred years ago, children were raised with the kind of reinforcement that comes most naturally to most humans – criticism for poor performance. If you misbehaved, you were cuffed, and that was that. Then, in 1938, B.F. Skinner wrote the first book on behaviorism, and the idea caught on. Over the next 35 years, he and others radically expanded the field of behavioral psychology and made one of the most influential discoveries of all time: that positive reinforcement is far more effective than negative reinforcement at producing the desired result.

Today, with corporal punishment illegal in most states and spanking children frowned upon by many, we've entered the second generation of the positive-feedback loop. That is, children are being raised in a positive-feedback environment by parents who were raised on positive feedback. The result is an arguable over-reliance on positive reinforcement in areas where it's not necessarily warranted.

A famous example, mentioned earlier, is the practice of giving everyone in a sports league a trophy, regardless of victory or defeat. Proponents claim that it rewards effort, while critics claim that it undermines the value of competition and discourages children from seeking to improve themselves.

I'm going to withhold my judgment. And then, I'm going to add some fuel to the fire.

CHANGES IN PARENTING STYLES

At the turn of the century, it was thought that coddling your baby was doing your child a disservice. Experts suggested feeding them on a regular schedule, leaving them to cry through the night and resisting picking up or hugging them, to better prepare a baby for the harsh realities of life.

A parent's job was to explain to their children how to behave, and then to enforce the rules of behavior, weeding out the "bad" ones.

It was 1946 when Dr. Benjamin Spock wrote *The Common Sense Book of Baby and Child Care*, which argued, for the first time, that parents should trust their instincts, and for example, feed their children. Radical at the time, moms liked being able to hug their babies, and that book has now sold over 50 million copies to date.

Other experts followed suit. A search on Amazon.com shows over 108,000 books on the subject of parenting. The following models are among the most common:

1. Nurturant – A parent's job is to let the child explore its surroundings, with constant nurturing and encouragement, as well as some (limited) protection.

2. Attachment – A strong emotional bond between parent and child will result in strong relationships later in life.

3. Taking Children Seriously – Rejects coercion and punishment and gives children responsibility from an early age. The fundamental principle is that it is possible to raise and educate children without parental self-sacrifice and without forcing the child to do anything against their will.

In all of these, children have far more control over their environment than in the traditional method of parenting, which leads me to the final swathe of gasoline to pour on the flame:

REDUCED ATTENTION SPAN

Remember letters? Those were messages that people wrote with actual pen and ink, in which they described what was going on in their lives.

Remember trains? We used to use them to travel across the country.

Remember books? Once upon a time, if you needed

information, you'd find a library and read one, using the Dewey Decimal System to find it.

This book has already discussed the world of technology rather extensively. Like it or not, we're in a fast-paced world with e-mail, airplanes and Internet search engines, which reduce the amount of time it takes to accomplish just about everything.

One effect of this is a need for instant gratification. Kids just can't handle waiting weeks to get feedback on something. There's no excuse for it, and by the time they get that feedback, they've lost interest.

So, with all that said, we get to the fire:

The Sum of All Parts

The cumulative effect of all of this is that by the time children reach school age, they're pretty much expecting to be rewarded and they're expecting to be rewarded now.

Kids come to school expecting something they'll enjoy, or at the very least, something for which they'll receive some kind of prize, and are instead met with homework, rules and grades. Instead of getting a trophy or candy for a job well done, they get detentions or trips to the principal's office for their failures. Where's the fun in that? Who wants to be stuck in that environment?

Since you're not their parents, your job isn't to undo the last five or fifteen years of this child's life, but to grow and develop the child you've got. Since these kids are used to getting rewarded for their efforts, your job is to reward them for their efforts. Since they were raised in an environment where they were getting constant attention, your job then becomes giving them that attention. And since they're used to getting all of that now, you need to give it to them now.

REWARDS FOR ALL

An elementary-school teacher I met used to give prizes to her children for answering questions right. These prizes weren't expensive. We're talking about fun-size candy bars or the trinkets you might find in the "25-cents-for-a-guaranteed-prize" vending games. Except she had a big box of them and would toss them (gently!) at her students when they answered a question right or when they did or said something else smart. The children got really into it and had fun while learning at the same time. Some students got more than others, but everyone who put in any effort at all would get something, thus rewarding effort and outstanding performance.

The funny thing is, she also taught an adult class for a year, with students ranging in age from 20 to 60. And she did the exact same thing with the exact same prizes, and got the exact same result. The adults knew that they would most likely just throw the prizes away at the end of the night, but still, they were eager to please, eager to have fun, eager to act like kids, and eager to be rewarded for their efforts.

The point is that rewards work, no matter how small or silly they are, and can actually be a path to intrinsic motivation.

Reread Chapter 5 for ideas on providing rewards that motivate students to work harder. The important thing to remember here is to reward everyone, not just the top performers, while at the same time looking for reward opportunities that push students to work harder.

Creating Long-Term Incentives

Of course, the flip side of giving them what they know is expanding their horizons. I've said before that part of your job as teacher is to push the students past their comfort zone, and their reward structure is no different. If a child is used to instant gratification, give them that, but also look for ways to create long-term incentives and reward long-term results. This is a necessary component of training a child for a real world in which you don't always get candy just for coming up with a good suggestion in a meeting.

Rewards for All with a Bonus for the Best

Here are some ideas on how to reward everyone for their effort, while still offering an incentive for students to work harder:

- *Give candy or a token prize for every question answered correctly in class.*
- *Publish the students' best essays in a bound book, and let the students vote on the best one(s), giving prizes to the winner(s).*
- *Every day, select a 'King of the Class,' based on performance or improvement, making sure to even the selections as much as possible. Look for excuses to boost the weaker students' confidence.*
- *Let one student per week work with you to develop next week's class.*

Step 1: Set Goals

In life, the biggest difference that separates the top performers from the rest of the field is the creation of clear goals with specific, measurable results. You, as a teacher, no doubt have some such goals for yourself. Getting all of your students to pass their standardized tests may be one.

Do your students have goals for themselves? In college classes – particularly in smaller classes in artistic subjects – it's very common for teachers to ask their students at the beginning of the year, why they're taking this class. As well as giving the teacher some information on what his students are looking to get out of this class (and thus helping him better engineer the direction or the exercise within the class), it empowers the student to give himself some direction, rather than just going with the flow and doing whatever the teacher tells him to.

Why not empower your students to do the same thing? Especially if you teach a class that students are required to take, letting them set goals for themselves puts them at choice and empowers them to learn. They now have something at stake for your class, they know what they can get, and they know what they're missing out on if they don't do the work.

Be *S.M.A.R.T.* when setting your goals:

Specific: "I want to be smarter," doesn't really tell you much. How do you want to be smarter? What do you want to be smarter at? Go into details about yourself and what you stand to gain out of the class.

Measurable: "I want to be the best running back of all time" is an admirable aspiration, but it doesn't really mean anything. What constitutes "best"? Most single-season rushing yards? Most career touchdowns? Winning the most Super Bowls? A sports commentator saying you're the best?

When Emmitt Smith was in college, he wrote down on a slip of paper that his goal was to be the NFL's all-time leading rusher. This was measurable: he knew, from the day he started that as soon as he ran for 16,727 yards, he would have broken Walter Payton's record and achieved his goal. In addition, he could tell, at every stage of his career, how close he was to meeting that goal. After seven seasons, he had rushed for 10,160 yards: right on track.

This is the difference between an aspiration and a measurable goal.

Attainable: A goal must be realistic and achievable; without that, it's not really a goal, it's a dream, at best. Having your goals be realistic and attainable is key to staying continually motivated to achieve them.

Relevant: A good history teacher knows that history isn't about the dates. If a student comes back with something like "I want to be able to hold a conversation with someone about the history of the United States," encourage him to move beyond that. Why does he want to be able to hold that conversation? What does he, personally, stand to gain from that?

Timely: The goal should be achievable within a reasonable, delineated timeframe.

STEP 2: CREATE REWARDS

Now that you and your students all know what they want out of the year, it's time to create some rewards.

The best rewards are obviously those that will increase the intrinsic value of the learning process. For that, you want something that's related to the goals and successes of your students. Pizza parties are fun, but field trips are fun and educational. The ideal rewards will hit both sides of the edutainment coin, and that's what you should strive for. And since the goals are measurable, the rewards can be set up at periodic intervals throughout the

141

school year when they're showing significant progress toward meeting those goals.

Here are a few ideas for rewards that meet these criteria:

- A field trip.
- A book on a topic that is relevant and interesting to them (e.g., *The Complete Works of Shakespeare* for an English class, *Anne Frank's Diary* for a history class, etc.).
- The choice of material for the next part of the semester.
- Create-your-own science experiment.
- A math puzzle game.

Whatever they are, make sure these rewards are bigger than the day-to-day instant gratification they receive, so they're clear that it was worth the effort they put in.

You can, on occasion, let your students know what these rewards are, and you can even involve them in the process. Knowing what's at stake both intrinsically and extrinsically may help motivate them. Be careful, though – if you set them up to expect something, then instead of being a reward when they get it, it'll be a punishment if they don't, and negative reinforcement isn't nearly as effective as positive. See Step 4 for more on this.

> *Only those who dare to fail greatly can ever achieve greatly.*
> *– Robert Francis Kennedy*

STEP 3: MONITOR PROGRESS

As you're monitoring the progress of your students inside the Theory C teaching model, look back regularly at the goals they gave you. How are they doing? Are they making progress toward them? If not, what needs to change? If necessary, give your students an opportunity to change the goals they've created for themselves – just make sure, when they do it, that it's coming from a place of empowerment and not from discouragement. The way to do this is:

1. Acknowledge the failure. Remember that failure is not a bad thing. The most successful people in life are those who failed often and didn't give up. So learn to accept and say, "I did not accomplish my goal," without any sense of negativity or wrong-doing.

2. Determine the cause of the failure. Look at what you did, and what was missing that caused you not to achieve your goal.

3. Brainstorm new ways to success for the future. Come up with as many new ideas as possible for future success.

4. Create new goals. If the goals were accomplished too easily, make them harder, and if they were not accomplished, make them a little bit easier. Also, as you're going through the school year, frequently referring back to these goals will help you to create lesson plans that play to their interests and goals, which in turn, boosts motivation and interest.

STEP 4: REWARD AS PROMISED

The final step is to issue the reward, although the far harder task is deciding not to issue the reward when that's the appropriate call.

If a student has come to expect a reward and he doesn't get it, his experience will be one of discipline. In essence, the recovery for this is similar to the Recovery Script from Chapter 4, but here we'll use the C.A.R.E. method.

1. Communicate the reasons for not giving the reward. Be honest! Don't sugar-coat it or just assume they know the reasons they're being "punished," but state the expectation that wasn't met, so they are clear on it.

2. Ask them what they could have done differently. Just like in the Recovery Script, this is a way to make them feel like they are a part of the solution, instead of just a part of the problem, and empowers them in moving forward.

3. Re-promise the reward. Offering them another shot at the reward reinforces the notion that good things in life are worth working for. Since they get another shot at it, the experience of punishment is lessened, and they'll know to work for it next time. Also, as part of this step, if their goals have proven to be more difficult to achieve than they anticipated, you may want to work with them to make them a little bit easier.

4. Encourage them by reminding them that the most successful people in life are those who failed often, but didn't give up.

By using the C.A.R.E. method, the students will be empowered to continue to work toward their goal.

THE COMMITMENT TREE

A commitment is different from a goal. Whereas goals are specific and measurable, a commitment is an expression of what you want in life. "Being the best running back in the world," starts to approach the territory of commitment, but even that isn't entirely accurate, because most running backs would be just as satisfied being the best quarterback in the world or being the best basketball player in the world. To be a renowned professional athlete, loved and respected by all – that's a commitment. It's a personal definition of success, and it's a great place to start, before identifying goals.

Think of it as a tree. What starts out as a simple seed, through nurturing and hard work, becomes a monumental legacy. And just like there are different kinds of trees – oak, birch, maple, and so on, each starting from a different kind of seed – every tree in itself is beautiful and unique.

THE SEED

To start building the commitment tree, have your students write down their "seed." This is the idea for what they want in life, what would have them be fulfilled. Don't worry too much about getting it right at this stage, because while the seed is the foundation, it's the parts that come next that really determine the seed's success.

TIPS FOR PLANTING THE SEED

- *Ask yourself why this is something that inspires you.*
- *Identify your definition of success and how your seed plays into that.*
- *Create short-term and long-term goals that are part of this commitment.*
- *Don't skip over this step. It's so easy to gloss over, but this is where the entire commitment starts. Having a clear definition will only serve you in the future.*

What comes next is to nourish and nurture the seed by giving it water and fertilizer. This, in terms of your commitment tree, is where we begin to explore why it is this particular idea that calls to you. What, really, do you want out of it? Is it to make money? Is it so that you can support a family? Is it so that you are remembered? Is it to make children happy? What is it about that seed that makes you want to pursue it?

So, take that simple gut reaction, the idea for what

147

your students want in life, and have them explore it further. If they say they want to be an astronaut, perhaps what's actually calling to them is a life of adventure. If they say they want to be president, maybe they want to change the world for the better.

By watering and fertilizing the seed, the tree can start to prepare itself for the journey it's about to take, and similarly, by having them write down their commitments, you are setting your students up for the training and education they will need to accomplish their commitment.

THE ROOTS

Before any tree breaks the surface and starts to grow towards the sky, it will spread a root system underground that will enable it to grow and become strong. The root system is actually larger than what we see above ground level. The stronger and more dynamic the root system, the taller the commitment tree will grow, and the same is true for a commitment.

TIPS FOR ESTABLISHING YOUR ROOTS SYSTEM

• *Know, ahead of time, what training and education will be necessary along the way.*
• *Resolve never to stop learning.*
• *Realize that this may not always be fun, and there may not be a lot of glory in it, but it's part of the process and well worth the effort.*
• *It doesn't have to be a drag! You can make it fun, if you choose to do so.*

Developing your roots means getting the necessary education and training, and adjusting your lifestyle, to accommodate this commitment. It means doing all the necessary work that you have to do, but don't want to do, because there's no glory in it whatsoever. Professional athletes work their tails off to get better, and without exception, it's the level of commitment that makes the difference between being a pro and not.

The Stem

Your hard work has paid off and your tree is starting to break ground. You're going in the right direction. Maybe you got that entry level job that you were looking for or that internship in the White House. All of your planning and preparation is paying off and you're starting to see the success of your commitment.

But you're not done yet. Any seed can sprout, but it really takes something to grow into a fully formed tree. The more you continue to learn, the thicker the tree trunk becomes, and the more prepared you are to survive trials and weather the elements.

As you continue to grow, you may need to revamp your game plan and develop strategies that will help you in your quest. These will necessarily be affected by your circumstances, but regardless of what they are, the harder you work and the more care you give yourself, the stronger you will become.

Branches

What started out as a seed or an idea has begun to blossom with more and more branches shooting out in different directions. Each branch in your tree represents opportunities, and as those opportunities flourish, they blossom with leaves.

> ### Tips for Growing the Stem
>
> • *Listen to your heart and trust your instincts.*
> • *Determination will be the only factor that will ensure your grip and allow you to continue to climb.*
> • *Continue your education.*
> • *Don't jump too soon. The branches of opportunity are in your sights, but jumping for them prematurely may leave you flat on your face and having to start over.*

Note that if you're still a seed, there are no branches. The opportunities don't come to those who haven't worked for it. Moreover, if a huge opportunity fell your way, and you were still just a weak little seed or a stem, you wouldn't know what to do with it, and the opportunity would just pass you by. It's the accumulation of experience and hard work that makes it possible for you to take advantage of these opportunities. That's why the first steps are so important.

> ## Tips for Building Branches
>
> • *Welcome change with open arms. Change brings about opportunity.*
> • *Look for new opportunities. Take on the challenge of climbing out on a new branch.*
> • *Invite risk into your game plan. If you happen to fail other branches will catch your fall.*

And the more opportunities you seize, the more branches you have, and before you know it, you're fifty feet tall and staring out over the world as a large, fully alive, lush and beautiful tree. Oak, birch, maple, or otherwise, you may look a little different than you expected, but the commitment is still the same, dictated entirely by the seed you nurtured from the very beginning

The Forest

A successful idea and a well-established commitment can grow far beyond one tree, though. Every forest started from one seed, and when a tree has grown, it is

> *The people who get on in this world are the people who get up and look for the circumstances they want, and if they can't find them, they make them.*
> *– George Bernard Shaw*

able to reproduce into something much more.

When an individual has found success, that success finds its way to everyone he touches, and the forest is the impact of that success, spread out to everyone he knows and loves.

THE LAZARUS TREE

Charles Lazarus came to the decision to open a children's furniture store after serving in World War II. All the veterans going home at the end of war were talking about how they wanted to raise a family, so he saw it as a business opportunity that would make him successful.

Lazarus was the son of a small business owner. His father had owned a bicycle repair shop, so Charles had experience building and repairing things, and he had experience running a business. This was the root system that enabled him, at the age of 25, to take this leap into owning his own business.

He used a few dollars he'd saved up to rent out the space his father's bicycle repair shop had been in, on the ground floor of the house in which he grew up. He sold cribs, strollers and other children's furniture needs, just like he'd planned, and his store began to turn a profit.

From this stem, he quickly realized that the key to success is listening to customer's needs, so when a customer came in looking for toys, he decided to start carrying a small stock of them. Soon, he noticed that the customers who bought toys would return for more, but the customers who bought furniture rarely did. So he

151

reversed his inventory selection, selling more toys than furniture.

Then, looking for ways to branch his business out even more (the toy market, in general, was beginning to grow like a wildfire), he saw that the supermarket next door had closed down, so he moved in there, lining the shelves with row upon row of toys, which he was now able to sell at a lower price because of the greater volume.

Lazarus' commitment, as you can see, was not to own a children's store, but to be a successful businessman. And he seized on every opportunity to grow his business. So when, in 1957, he had saved up enough money for a second store, he opened up the world's first Toys "R" Us. By 1966, he had four stores, and by 1997, Toys "R" Us had grown into a forest of 811 superstores, all from just a tiny little seed.

Seeing the Forest for the Trees

Isn't it amazing how long a tree can live? And isn't it amazing, how the longer it lives, the stronger it grows? If a well-established tree is struck by lightning, part of it may break off, but any part left standing will continue to grow, even if it has to grow sideways.

That is true for humans and their relationships with life. Many of us will be hit by some extraordinary circumstance, and such inevitabilities will cause some to falter, but if you are truly committed to your game plan, you can withstand any storm, and you can stand up to almost any attack.

In short, the more dedicated you become, the greater your chance of survival.

This is a lesson worth teaching your students, because right now, they're still seeds. Treated right, you will have a forest of success before you in your future.

But, that all starts with a little bit of water and a little bit of care to prepare them for the world to come.

Key Points to Remember

• *Spurred by behavioral psychology, technology and changes in parenting styles, kids are looking for immediate positive feedback to motivate them to move forward.*

• *Make sure to include long-term incentives to teach students that good things come with hard work and dedication.*

• *Set goals, and be* **S.M.A.R.T.** *when doing so: make your goals* **S***pecific,* **M***easurable,* **A***ttainable,* **R***elevant and* **T***imely.*

• *Create rewards that have both intrinsic and extrinsic value.*

• *Monitor progress, making sure to re-empower for any failures by* **acknowledging the failure, determining the cause, brainstorming new ways for success and creating new goals.**

• *Reward as promised, using* **C.A.R.E.** *for rewards not given:* **C***ommunicate the reasons for not giving the reward;* **A***sk what they could have done differently;* **R***e-promise the reward; and offer words of* **E***ncouragement.*

• *A commitment is a personal definition of success. Teach your students to grow their commitments like a tree, establishing a grounded and nourished seed, growing a roots system with education, establishing a strong trunk and then seizing opportunities like branches.*

153

Chapter 8
Check That
Attitude

Watching that Attitude

A Dash of Diversity ...

The United States is a country born on immigration.

In the 1840s and 50s, it was Irish and German. After the Civil War, they started coming from southern and eastern Europe, a trend that lasted for a good hundred years or more, by which time, Hispanic and East-Asian immigration started to grow.

In all of that time, immigration was resisted, and it continues to be resisted today. But of all the people

155

resisting it, the one demographic not bothered by the steady rise of the immigrant population is young people.

Perhaps part of the reason is exposure. Once upon a time, the only exposure you had to someone of a different race or background was through hearsay or through an unfortunate clash with someone from a neighboring borough. The Italian-Americans stuck to Little Italy, the Chinese-Americans stuck to Chinatown, and as long as they didn't cross paths, everyone was happy.

But the American melting pot has softened those boundaries, so people encounter, on a daily basis, people of different races or religions. They've watched Chappelle's Show on Comedy Central and they saw Barack Obama run for President and win. Interracial marriages are ten times more common than they were even 30 years ago.

Interracial Marriages

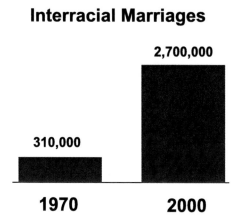

Even beyond that, they've had the Internet to expose them to the rest of the world. Play "Internet Hearts" on your computer, and the chat box will tell you what language your opponents speak. Go to YouTube, and it takes seconds to find footage of some crazy Japanese game show. Get onto a discussion forum and people from all over the world are asking and answering questions.

Airplanes make travel quicker and easier, so where, 60 or 70 years ago, only the wealthiest American businessmen might have traveled to Europe or Asia over the course of their lifetimes, international vacationing is now a popular and oft-achieved goal among middle class families.

In 1994, 76,000 Americans participated in some sort of study abroad program. In 2004, that number was up to 191,000.

In short, the world has gotten smaller, and Gen-Nexters want to see it.

... with a Smattering of Cynicism

On the flip side, 30 years ago parents took their three-year-olds to the community playground or swimming pool and left them there for two hours while they ran errands. After all, with other parents watching, the kids couldn't get into too much trouble. People were generally good, and you just trusted them.

But media coverage of violence has exploded over the past several decades, and regardless of any actual changes in crime, that just doesn't happen today. From the time they're born, parents and children alike believe that it's a big bad world where all kinds of nasty things could happen, which means that children are conditioned, from birth, to be skeptical of the world around them.

157

After being taught not to take candy from strangers, they watched their parents react to the collapse of Enron and learned that businesses are corrupt. Then, they learned about Watergate and realized you can't trust politicians either. Then, they watched *Bowling for Columbine* and learned that violence has actually **gone down** over the last 30 years, but it's **media coverage** of violence that's gone up – which means you can't trust the media either.

And let's not forget that half of them are from divorced families, which carries with it its own set of trust issues. So, by the time they're teens they've corroborated for themselves what their parents taught them as children; it's a big, bad world and you can't trust anybody.

Satisfying the Cynical Optimist

Dealing with this attitude isn't difficult, it's just a matter of understanding the world these kids grew up in and treating them with respect. Kids hate being treated like kids, so the trick is, effectively, to treat them just like you would treat any adult.

1. Be honest and open. Never lie to one of your students. Never pretend that you know the answer when you don't. If they don't trust you, there's no way they can learn from you. And expanding on that, the more open you are and willing to discuss whatever is on their minds, the more they're willing to trust and respect you.

2. Remain neutral on controversial issues. Not too long ago, people were taught that there were topics you don't discuss in polite company: race, religion and politics were at the top of that list, and continue to be controversial subjects today. It actually isn't a bad idea for you to engage in intelligent discussions on those topics with your students – after all, they're exposed to all of these things, and discuss them regularly among themselves, so having such a discussion with a well-educated expert such as yourself offers new opportunities for new perspectives.

But anytime you discuss a controversial issue you run the risk of alienating someone who disagrees with you. And you don't want to alienate your students, which is why it's so important to maintain a neutral stance.

The rule is that if you find yourself criticizing or judging someone or something, or if you find yourself trying to convince someone of something, then you're probably not remaining neutral. People shut down when they feel like they're being made wrong for their opinion, and that goes doubly so for kids. So let everyone speak their mind, and be the moderator, rather than the judge.

3. Look for ways to break cultural barriers. This book has spent a fair bit of time discussing the importance of technology in today's classroom, but not everyone has access to this technology. Students in poor districts may not have cell phones or computers or Tivo, and may resent those who do. This becomes more difficult to endure if they live in a district with split income levels or split cultures, and it becomes more difficult still if they're the one person who's different from the rest – the poor kid at the rich school or the white kid in the black class.

When creating your lessons, it's imperative to be sensitive to these differences and to look for ways to break these barriers. Do not require students to deliver an assignment in a way that's impossible for them to deliver. And if it's more difficult for them than their classmates, for whatever reason, try to make it easier. Seek them out, as you do all your students (since you're a Theory C teacher) and give them what they need to feel comfortable to fit in or grow with the rest of the class. Without embarrassing anyone, show the majority what life outside their little bubble is like – not in a cursory way, but through some kind of project or lesson that really gets to the heart of how uncomfortable life can be.

A great way to do this is to tie lessons into current events. You're studying the Great Depression? Show some abject poverty that's in a ghetto a little closer to home. Your students will feel much more connected to something that's going on right now, five or fifty miles away from where they live than they will to something that happened 70 or 80 years ago. That's five to ten times as long as they've been alive – so long, they can't even fathom it.

Really, what all of this amounts to, is exposing students, as much as possible, to other people and cultures, which is an education that most of them desperately crave.

4. Teach them to follow their dreams. This is a generation that thoroughly believes that they can accomplish anything they set their minds to. They believe this, and they desperately want validation for this belief. They want to know that the only things holding them back are themselves and the old people telling them otherwise. You must not be one of these people.

It is a big, bad, scary world out there, but it's only made more so by negativity and regret, and Generation Next wants no part of that. They know that it was the world's dreamers who made men fly; that it was a man who never gave up who invented the light bulb; that the person who told the world we would put a man on the moon had no idea how it would be done; and that the person who won eight gold medals worked longer and harder than everyone else in the sport.

Teach them to follow their dreams. Because more than anything else, that is your job as a teacher of Generation Next.

This above all, to thine own self be true.
– William Shakespeare

Key Points to Remember

• *With the world getting smaller, Generation Next has more direct exposure to people of different cultures and backgrounds than any other generation. This makes them far more open to diversity than any other generation in history.*

• *By the same token, they've been conditioned from youth to be cynical about the world around them.*

• *To satisfy the cynical optimist, **be open and honest** in your communications, remain neutral on controversial issues, **look for ways to break cultural barriers** and **teach them to follow their dreams.***

A Story of Empowerment

It was the last day of my junior year of high school. With 5 minutes left before the bell rang, we were counting down the seconds before we were out the door and off to a summer of fun.

I remember sitting on my desk, talking to my friends, when the door opened to the classroom, catching everyone's attention. An office aide walked toward my teacher, carrying one of those pink "come to the office" slips that I had known so well. She handed it to my teacher, everyone watching to see who was being called down to the office with only a few minutes left before the end of the year.

"This better not be me," I thought.

My teacher looked up, stared straight at me with a smile and said, "Bryan, you are the lucky one."

"Not again ..."

My friends all snickered, and then started laughing as I literally sprinted out of the room to the principal's office. I wanted to get this over with as soon as possible – I had no desire to miss even a single minute of my summer break.

I arrived at the office, and the principal's secretary greeted me with a smile. "We've been waiting for you, she said."

"Who's 'we?'" I wondered. Peeking my head into Mrs. Collier's office, I saw my father sitting there with a big smile on his face. This, I knew, was not good.

"Bryan, please sit down," Mrs. Collier said.

"No, I'll stand," I responded. "The bell's about to ring – I have places to go and people to see."

With a smirk, she placed her hand on my back and said, "Please sit down, this might take a while." The bell rang, and the screams and whistles started to fill the hallway and the lawn outside Mrs. Collier's office, as my classmates took off for parties. I looked at my father and back at my principal, and then reluctantly took a seat.

"Bryan, we are here today to give you an award."

"What?" I said, shocked. "An award? Can't this wait until next year? I have people waiting for me."

"No," she said, "We need to give it to you now. We are here this afternoon to commend you on your writing abilities."

I was a little confused. On the one hand, I was glad to

finally be getting some respect around here, but behind all that I was thinking, "Really? I didn't know I was such a great writer."

Then the bomb dropped. My principal reached down and pulled out a folder that contained a stack of 31 forged notes that dismissed me from school. She gave me a look that said, "Gotcha!" My throat sank into my stomach as I looked over at my dad, wondering what kind of trouble I'd be in now.

She then pulled out a sheet of paper and slid it across the desk and said, "Sign this. Sign it and you'll never have to come to school again."

I thought, "Seriously, it's that easy?"

She continued, "You obviously don't like school, so this is your chance to have the endless summer vacation as a high school drop-out."

The word "drop-out" didn't sit well with me. I looked over at my dad, the person who has always told me to work hard in school, get good grades and be a success in life. "Sign it," he said. My head was spinning. "We've never had a loser in the family, so this might be neat."

There was a long, awkward pause as I looked back and forth between my father, my principal and the drop-out slip she'd placed in front of me. "They can't really be serious," I thought.

Finally, Mrs. Collier broke the silence and said, "I tell you what. This is a big decision. You take this form home, and if you decide to sign it, just put a stamp on and send it back and you're done.

"But if you do decide to come back to finish your senior year,

*you cannot miss one day of school or we **will kick you out.**
No questions asked. You can't even miss one class,
period." She lowered her voice and moved closer to me, looking
me straight in the eyes. "You're a gifted student and a born
leader, Bryan. I believe in you. It's extraordinary that you
managed to pass all your classes, considering you missed half
the school year. Image what you can do for yourself if you
actually show up. Imagine what you could become in life if you
committed yourself 100% to whatever you set out to do."*

*I left that afternoon thinking not about the parties or my
friends or my plans for the summer, but about what I would do
next year and for the rest of my life. All summer long, I
couldn't get my principal's words out of my head. "Imagine
what you can do for yourself if you actually show up."*

*I did decide to show up my senior year, and at the end of the
year, I was voted "Most Improved Student" by my
classmates. I didn't miss a single day of class until my senior
year of college.*

*That afternoon, my principal changed the course of my life
forever. Her simple words of encouragement have stayed with
me after all these years, and ultimately, shaped my career path
as a speaker to reach out and help others, just as she did for me.*

*Go back and think about why you become a teacher. I'm
willing to bet that you signed up because you, too, wanted to
make a difference in the lives of children. We have all had that
teacher that made us feel special and impacted our lives beyond
the scope of understanding, and as an educator, you truly have
the ability to touch the lives of children everyday, even more so
than their own parents.*

*The reality of life is that you're lucky if you get one or two
students in your career who will come back and tell you about*

the difference you made. I never told my principal before she passed away in 1999. Maybe her spirit is what keeps the fire burning inside me to reach out and help others. I almost feel as if I owe it her. That's why you have to really want it. That's why, above all, you have to love working with children.

Your children show up to school motivated and excited. They look their teachers in the eyes and say to themselves, "I hope you are the one that will set me free." My best advice to you is to let this information sink in. Start working on one skill per week in the classroom. This generation will keep you wondering and on your toes, I promise. And remember, the real secret to happiness in life is to give back to others. You're living that each and every day. Keep up the good fight!

ABOUT THE AUTHOR
BRYAN FIESE

Bryan Fiese, a dynamic speaker, says the dependence kids have on technology is causing a lack of interpersonal communication skills. He offers insights to understand this generation and clear, effective methods to connect and motivate.

Bryan's upbeat message, charisma and humor will leave audiences both informed and inspired as he shares this information and so much more.

CREDENTIALS:

Bryan Fiese, co-founder of Motivated Proformance Inc, is a speaker with a background in education, training, marketing and management. His seminar/workshop is used by schools around the U.S. for training teachers. Bryan has appeared on national TV and radio and presented to millions at conferences, workshops and training events. Author of several books, his latest is *NO TEACHER LEFT BEHIND: Keeping Up With and Captivating "Generation Next" In the Classroom.*

From heads of major companies to full-time students, Bryan's upbeat messages are very popular! His audiences leave with big smiles, increased energy and inspiration due to his humor and charisma.

Quick Order Form

Telephone Orders: 866-465-7073
E-mail: susie@getumotivated.com
Fax Orders: 512-535-1996
Online Orders: www.getumotivated.com
Postal Orders: Motivated Proformance, Inc.
628 Canyon Rim Dr.
Dripping Springs, TX 78620

Name: _____

Address:_____

_____

_____

City:_____ State:_____

Zip Code:_____

Telephone:_____

Email:_____

Sales Tax: Please add 8.25% for orders shipped
toTexas addresses.
Shipping: $3.85 for the first book and $2.00 for each
additional book.
Call for information on staff development,
conferences and workshops.